Community, anarchy and liberty

Community, Anarchy and Liberty

MICHAEL TAYLOR

Reader in Government
University of Essex

CAMBRIDGE UNIVERSITY PRESS

CAMBRIDGE
LONDON   NEW YORK   NEW ROCHELLE
MELBOURNE   SYDNEY

Published by the Press Syndicate of the University of Cambridge
The Pitt Building, Trumpington Street, Cambridge CB2 1RP
32 East 57th Street, New York, NY 10022, USA
296 Beaconsfield Parade, Middle Park, Melbourne 3206, Australia

First Published 1982

Printed in Great Britain at the University Press, Cambridge

Library of Congress catalogue card number: 82-1173

British Library cataloguing in publication data
Taylor, Michael
Community, anarchy and liberty.
1. Anarchism and anarchists
I. Title
335'.83   HX833

ISBN 0 521 24621 0 hard covers
ISBN 0 521 27014 6 paperback

Selections have been used from the following works:
Anarchy and Cooperation by M. Taylor. Copyright© 1976 John Wiley and Sons Ltd.
Reprinted by permission of John Wiley and Sons Ltd.
Anarchy, State and Utopia by Robert Nozick. Copyright© 1974 by Basic Books Inc.
By permission of Basic Books Inc., Publishers, New York, and Basil Blackwell, Oxford.
Philosophy, Science and Method, by S. Morgenbesser, P. Suppes and M. White. By permission of St Martin's Press Inc.

Contents

Acknowledgements

Earlier versions of parts of this book were presented at the conferences on 'Anarchism and Law' at the Erasmus University of Rotterdam and on 'The Theory of a Free Society' at Oxford in 1979, and at the ECPR workshop on 'Liberty' at Florence in 1980. Conversations with participants in these meetings and their criticisms of my contributions have been helpful and are gratefully acknowledged. I should also like to thank those friends who have discussed the ideas of this book with me and the readers for Cambridge University Press for their helpful comments on the manuscript. The bulk of the book was written during a year's leave of absence from the University of Essex when I was financially supported by an SSRC Personal Research Grant, for which I am most grateful.

1

Anarchy and community

I set out in the studies which have resulted in this book to discover whether anarchy – doing without the state – is viable and, if so, what sort of anarchy that would be and whether it was compatible with certain fundamental ideals of communitarian anarchists and other socialists, notably those of liberty and equality.

It seemed to me that the critical test of the viability of anarchy was whether its members could maintain social order, in the basic sense of security of persons and their property (however much or little property there is). Most writers in the communitarian anarchist tradition do not recognise this as a problem for the anarchies they desire or predict for the future, where it would be solved or obviated by a transformed human nature, appropriately socialised. But the maintenance of social order has always been a problem, in every kind of society, even in those where private property or possession is limited to the barest, easily replaceable goods; and there are no grounds for the anarchists' optimism that the problem would resolve itself as effortlessly as they suppose even in societies of the sort they envisage. When I speak of it as a problem, I mean that individuals will not voluntarily refrain from doing those things which threaten social order. The reason for this (as I argue in Section 2.1) is that there is an important element of social order which is a 'public good', that is to say a good which (roughly speaking) benefits every member of the public regardless of whether he contributes in any way to its provision. If a good is public in this sense an individual may be tempted to be a 'free rider', to benefit from whatever amount of the good others provide without contributing himself; and if many people attempt to be free riders little or none of the public good will be provided.

It is this problem about the provision of the public good of social order which justifies the state, in the view of many people. Of course, only a minimal state is justified, a 'night-watchman' state whose only functions are the maintenance of internal order and external defence (which is also a public good). In an earlier work, *Anarchy and Cooperation*, I argued that this way of justifying the state, even a minimal state, is fundamentally flawed. Here (in Section 2.2) I summarise very briefly the parts of that argument which are relevant to my present argument.[1]

Without the state, how is social order to be maintained? One answer is that the goods and services which go to make up social order can and should be provided by private firms competing in the marketplace. This 'libertarian' or anarcho-capitalist approach is currently enjoying a revival, espccially in the United States. In Section 2.3 I shall contend that social order cannot satisfactorily be put on the market, and in the remainder of Chapter 2 I shall argue instead that in the absence of the state social order can be maintained only if relations between people are those characteristic of *community*.

Community has largely been ignored in recent political theory. It is a horribly 'open-textured' concept, that is to say there is not and there cannot be an exhaustive specification of the conditions for its correct use. But there are what we might

---

[1] This brief section and a few pages on public goods in Section 2.1 are the only areas of overlap between the earlier book and the present one.

call core characteristics of community, attributes possessed in *some* degree by *all* communities, and among these are the requirements that relations between members of a community be direct and many-sided and that they practise certain forms of reciprocity (Section 1.4). Community is central to my whole argument. The book is therefore a book about socialism, if 'socialism' is taken, as I think it should be, to be primarily about the quality of relations between people, and only about the right kinds of ownership and distribution of resources (or anything else) insofar as these are necessary to relationships of the desired kind.

A very rough equality of basic material conditions is one of the necessary conditions of community. But according to a traditional argument, even an approximate economic equality would not survive for long in the absence of the state. If this is so, then anarchy, which (according to my argument in Chapter 2) depends on community, is not viable. The survival of equality in an anarchy is the subject of Chapter 3.

Egalitarian anarchic communities did in fact survive for millennia. *Homo sapiens* lived in such communities for nearly all of his forty or fifty thousand years. But eventually – in most cases during the last few centuries – they all but disappeared: absorbed, undermined or destroyed by states. How and why this happened throws an interesting light on the vulnerability of the egalitarian anarchic community and on the future prospects for a durable anarchy. This is the subject of Section 3.3.

The small, stable community which is at the centre of my argument is nowhere in this book assumed to be good or right in any sense; it is nowhere defended as an ideal, or viewed as a happy and continuously harmonious place, free from conflict or from constraint and coercion. The contention is simply that community is *necessary* – if people are to live without the state. But I do defend community (in Chapter 4) against the claim,

made especially by liberal writers, that it is incompatible with
or even inimical to individual liberty. This view is no more
accurate than the contrary one, which is little more than an
assumption in the writings of many communitarian anarchists
and other socialists, that liberty is possible only in community.

For evidence and illustration, I draw on the experience of
stateless 'primitive' communities and of quasi-anarchic 'intentional' communities and peasant communities of the closed,
corporate kind, for these constitute the chief, almost the only
empirical cases of anarchy and quasi-anarchy. But my argument
about the necessity of community is meant to apply to the
present and future as well. If we want to do without the state or
substantially reduce its role, we have to revive and rebuild
communities. What does this mean, and what are the possibilities
for such a renewal, in a crowded world of powerful states? I try
to answer this question in the final chapter.

1.2 Anarchy: what it is

The twin notions at the centre of this study, then, are 'anarchy'
and 'community'. Since there are no ready-made standard
usages of either of these terms, I need first to give some
explanation of how I shall be using them.

I have said that anarchy is, roughly speaking, a condition of
statelessness. I want now to modify this first approximation
and tighten it up, and I shall do this in a way that frees 'anarchy'
from dependence on an account of the 'state' as a list of specific
types of institutions (and criteria concerning their articulation
as a centralised system and the differentiation and autonomy of
the system itself) and at the same time in a way that prepares
the ground for the discussion (in Section 3.3) of the emergence
of the state.

My starting point is Max Weber's well-known definition of
states as 'human associations that successfully claim the mon-

opoly of legitimate use of physical force within a given territory'. Either as a necessary or as a sufficient condition for the existence of a state, this clearly won't do. *Claiming* the monopoly of the legitimate use of physical force (which, admittedly, states do – well-developed states at any rate) entails nothing about the actual possession of means of exercising force. Any group can claim a monopoly of the use of force or of the legitimate use of force, but this does not make it a state.[2] To be a state, it must actually possess at least some means of exercising force. So Weber is right to require that this claim must be successful. But then his test is far too stringent; and no instances of a state in this sense could be found. Obviously states never do possess an *actual* monopoly of the use of force (there are always individuals and often organised groups, other than those which are part of the state system, which continue to use force, even under a powerful, highly developed state), and presumably this is not what Weber meant by a 'successful' claim. But nor could a claim to a monopoly of *legitimate* use of force ever be fully successful in the sense that everyone or nearly everyone granted the state legitimacy.

What is left of the Weberian account is the notion of a concentration of force and the attempt by those in whose hands it is (incompletely) concentrated to determine who else shall be permitted to employ force and on what occasions. Both of these elements, it seems to me, *are* characteristic of states. The first is obviously basic, and I shall say that a minimum test, a necessary condition, for the existence of a state is that there is *some* concentration of the means of using force, or equivalently some inequality in its distribution. (How much concentration or inequality is a question I shall leave open.)[3] Conversely, in a

[2] Robert Nozick, *Anarchy, State and Utopia* (Oxford: Blackwell, 1974), p. 23.
[3] In my view it cannot be specified independently of other characteristics of the state. Whether a given degree of concentration of force suffices would depend in a particular case on the extent to which other criteria were

pure anarchy force is perfectly dispersed, not concentrated at all.

If pure anarchy requires that there be no inequality at all in the distribution of the means of using force or of the actual use of force, then no historical example of a perfectly anarchic society could be found and none is likely to be found in the future. The closest approximations are those primitive societies described by anthropologists as 'stateless' or 'acephalous' or even 'anarchic' (as in Evans-Pritchard's description of Nuer society as an 'ordered anarchy'). In these societies, the use of force is widely dispersed, but not perfectly so. Typically, those males who are neither too young nor too old to fight (the 'warriors') use force – and are expected by the community to use it – more than other groups: usually, they alone are charged with the defence of the society against external enemies, and in some of these societies it is a group consisting of close male kin of fighting age ('the vengeance group') which is responsible for coming to the defence of an aggrieved person and which in particular must exact vengeance if one of their members is killed. So in these societies there is *some* concentration of force, an inequality based on differences of sex and age. But the concentration goes no further than that and it is *ad hoc* in use. There is no standing, specialist group or organisation or centralised system of groups which possesses or endeavours to possess a monopoly on the use of force and the right to license its use, no group which has absorbed or aspires to absorb the rights of individuals or of 'vengeance groups' to use force in their pursuit of 'self-help' justice. Furthermore, even where, in societies of this kind, some individuals or groups have more influence on collective decisions than others – where disputes are settled with the help of a third-party mediator, for example,

satisfied. But I would argue that necessary and sufficient conditions for the existence of a state cannot be specified, because 'the existence of a state' is an open-textured concept. The notion of an open-textured concept is explained in a later section.

or where policies are decided by the elders – their decisions cannot be enforced; they are not backed up by the threat of force and have only the status of advice and recommendation (though their advice is usually followed, because it is deemed to be 'authoritative', in a sense I shall specify later).

In many bands of hunters and gatherers, the *de facto* use of force may be even less concentrated, because both internal violence (as in the pursuit of vengeance) and fighting with other societies are rare.

I have said that a necessary condition for a *pure* anarchy is that there is no concentration of force at all. A society of the sort I have just described, where there is a limited concentration of force but no means of enforcing collective decisions, is the closest empirical approximation and I shall call it an *anarchy*.

Some anthropologists have been unwilling to concede that even primitive societies of this kind are anarchies. This is because they give a functional account of the state, characterising it by what it importantly does, and then argue that since these things get done in all primitive societies, including the alleged anarchies, they cannot after all be anarchic or stateless. (Or sometimes a weaker claim is made that they are not without government or not without law.) In particular, it is pointed out (correctly) that the most basic function of the state is to ensure that internal social order is maintained (possibly so that extraction can continue smoothly to the benefit of a dominant class – I leave this question open); and since all primitive societies have means of maintaining order none of them can be anarchic. (On this account of the matter presumably a society would become anarchic when order broke down, so that 'anarchy' is identified, as it is popularly and journalistically, with disorder and chaos.) Bicycles and motor cars can be lumped together because they have the same basic function, but there are differences between them which are interesting from certain points of view (the bicycle is thermodynamically more efficient than the car, is less destructive of people and environment and community, and so on). So too are there differences between societies with a state (in the non-functional sense) and those which maintain order (or defend themselves or redistribute resources) by other means, and these differences are what I am interested in here.

There is another reason why it could be denied that some or even all of the primitive societies of the kind I take to be anarchic are in fact not so, namely that some individuals or groups in them play political roles and others do not. For example, in many of these societies there is a role occupied by an individual who alone acts as a mediator between parties in dispute, or a group – the elders, say – which acts as a court and also perhaps as a rudimentary kind of legislative assembly. These are examples of what I shall call a *division of political labour* or *political specialisation*. For such a division to exist, there must be political roles – positions which are recognised and enduring though possibly (in primitive societies, always) part-time, and which play a part in the maintenance of internal social order, dispute settlement and other collective decision-making, defence of the community, and redistribution of resources within the community. In chiefdoms (to be described in a later section), the chief occupies such a role; but individuals whose advice is sought and heeded simply because they are believed to possess superior skills or wisdom or knowledge do not occupy political roles.

I have referred to only one kind of division of political labour, namely the differentiation between those members of the society who play political roles and those who do not. This is the fundamental division and the only one relevant to a characterisation of 'anarchy'. But note that the development of this sort of political specialisation – the progressive exclusion of parts of the population from the political arena – tends to proceed hand in hand with two other (closely related but not ñecessarily identical) kinds of division of political labour; the first kind differentiates political roles from each other and the second makes roles functionally more specific.[4]

Empirically, and unsurprisingly, political specialisation tends to develop together with the process of monopolisation of force (though the correlation is far from perfect); but as we shall see in Section 3.3 when we look at the origin of the state, the division of political labour can develop considerably before there is any further monopolisation of force beyond concentration in the hands of adult males. Just as long as the occupants of the political roles which emerge in the early development of political specialisation are not backed by organised force, so cannot enforce their decisions throughout the community, I shall say we are still dealing with a stateless society. Nevertheless, since the ideal of some anarchist writers is a society in which force concentration *and* political specialisation are both at a minimum, and since it *is* useful to emphasise that anarchies vary greatly with respect to the degree of political specialisation, I shall say that the absence of any concentration of force and the absence of any political specialisation together constitute necessary and sufficient conditions for a *pure anarchy*.

This characterisation of 'anarchy' (only a limited degree of concentration of force) and 'pure anarchy' (no force concentration and no political specialisation) does not entail that movement away from the ideal of pure anarchy toward the formation and further development of a state can be measured by some variable – call it 'stateness' – which is a monotonically increasing function (holding other things constant) of concentration and of specialisation over the whole range of these two variables. It is not clear that, at least beyond a certain stage in its development, the state becomes ever more effective with

---

[4] Compare David Easton, 'Political anthropology', in B. J. Siegel, ed., *Biennial Review of Anthropology 1959* (Stanford: Stanford University Press, 1959).

increasing concentration of force at the centre and with increasing political specialisation. Some degree of dispersion, affording divisions and local units of the state partial autonomy and hence a measure of flexibility in dealing with local conditions, may enhance the overall control and extractive capability of the state.

Nevertheless, we can say that, to the extent that a society lacks political specialisation and to the extent that force is dispersed, to that extent also must there be *equal participation* in whatever political functions remain. All societies, including anarchies, use social controls of some kind to maintain social order; they redistribute resources amongst their members; and they make collective decisions; nearly all societies also defend or make preparations to defend themselves against actual or imagined external enemies and competitors. In an anarchy, there must be wide participation in all these activities.

Seen in this light – as a society in which there is equal, extensive participation – the anarchy I am interested in is not far from the political association which Rousseau's 'social contract' was to found. Only in a participatory political order of this kind do individuals owe political obligations and they owe them not to a state but to each other.[5]

1.3 Power, authority and what anarchy is not

Anarchist writers themselves have not been given to careful analysis of concepts, even those which are central to their systems of ideas. Some of them (and a few other writers too) have defined or written of anarchy as simply an absence of power or coercion or authority, or as an equality of one of these things. This has provided opportunities and excuses for all

---

[5] On Rousseau's radical break with the 'fraudulent liberal social contract', see Carole Pateman's excellent book, *The Problem of Political Obligation: A Critical Analysis of Liberal Theory* (London: Wiley, 1979).

manner of feeble criticism (beginning perhaps with Engels' piece 'On authority'), which is usually misplaced since the anarchists, at least the classical anarchist writers like Proudhon, Bakunin and Kropotkin, are concerned mainly with *doing without the state* and with forms of political and social organisation which would displace the state. These forms would not, and could not, entail the complete disappearance or equality of power, or coercion, or authority. The reasons for this are fairly straightforward (and will emerge later in this section and in later chapters), so would not perhaps require the digression which follows giving some account of the concepts of power, coercion, authority and other ways of getting people to do things they otherwise would not do. But since these concepts play a part in other phases of the book's argument, I had better make quite clear which of the competing accounts I shall be making use of.

There are a number of ways of getting people to do things, involving quite different processes, and the important thing is not what they are to be called but subdividing them so as not to obliterate or obscure these differences or to obstruct analysis. I shall subdivide them into power (treating coercion as a subclass of the ways in which power can be exercised), force or physical constraint, persuasion, the activation of commitments, and authority. Of these, the first and last are referred to most often in later chapters, so will be given a fuller account.

One of the ways in which one person can get another to pursue a course of action he would not otherwise have chosen to pursue is by affecting the incentives facing him, so that it is rational for him to choose this course of action. I call this the exercise of *power*. Power as a *possession* is the ability to affect incentives in this way. Prominent among the ways in which incentives may be changed so as to make a course of action the rational one to pursue are: rendering the course of action more desirable by attaching to it a promise or *offer* of a reward; rendering the course of action less desirable by attaching to it the *threat* of a penalty; and issuing a combination of a threat and offer, which (following Hillel Steiner) I shall call a *throffer*. A throffer takes the form of promising a reward if some course of action is chosen and threatening a penalty if it is not.

Of the few writers who have given an account of power in these rational-choice terms, most appear to restrict the exercise of power to the issuing of threats, offers and throffers or to threats alone.[6] But offers, threats and throffers are not the only means by which the incentives facing others may be altered. In many situations of interdependent decision-making, an individual may induce another to act differently merely by giving him reasons to believe that he himself will choose a particular course of action, which need not correspond to imposing positive or negative sanctions contingently upon the other's behaviour. In situations of interdependent decision-making

[6] The most comprehensive rational-choice account of power, an account which is not restricted to a consideration of threats, offers and throffers, is that given by John Charlton in his PhD dissertation on 'Political power' (University of Essex, 1978). It could be argued that this conception of power is implicit in the Theory of Games, though few game theorists have discussed power explicitly. An important exception is John Harsanyi. See his 'Measurement of social power, opportunity costs, and the theory of two-person bargaining games' and 'Measurement of social power in *n*-person reciprocal power situations', both in *Behavioral Science*, 7 (1962), 67–92. Brian Barry's otherwise excellent discussion of power is confined to threats and offers ('Power: an economic analysis', in B. Barry, ed., *Power and Political Theory: Some European Perspectives*, London: Wiley, 1976). Peter Bachrach and Morton S. Baratz, in their well-known articles on power (see their *Power and Poverty*, New York: Oxford University Press, 1970) use 'power' in a narrow and a broad sense. In the narrow usage, it is restricted to securing compliance through the issuing of credible threats. In the broad usage, power is treated as the ability of an individual to get his way in decision-making or to restrict the scope of decision-making to issues which are unimportant to him. I share John Charlton's reservations about the inadequacies of this second conception (see his 'Political power', sec. I). Steven Lukes appears to be content to accept this account in terms of decision-making and 'non-decision-making' as one of the dimensions of his 'three-dimensional' view of power (*Power: A Radical View*, London: Macmillan, 1974). Nowhere do Bachrach and Baratz and Lukes given an account of ways of affecting incentives other than by making threats.

among more than two individuals, the incentives facing one individual may be altered when others agree to cooperate, even when the courses of action they agree to pursue do not involve the making of threats and offers (whether explicitly or tacitly). Again, if power may be possessed only by individuals who are able to make credible threats and offers, then it would not be possible to make ascriptions of power to individuals in situations of interdependent decision-making who do not have threat or offer strategies available to them but who nevertheless are able, in virtue of their strategic position (that is, in virtue of the courses of action available to all the parties involved and of their preferences amongst the possible outcomes), to bring about outcomes relatively favourable to themselves and unfavourable to the others, by means of rational choices made on the assumption that the others will also choose rationally. An account of power which restricts its exercise to the issuing of threats and offers suffers also from the difficulty in some cases of determining whether or not a particular course of action is a threat (or offer).

I have said at the outset that power is the ability to affect the incentives facing others so that it becomes rational for them to pursue a certain course of action. But in what does this ability consist, if it is not to be restricted to the ability to make credible threats and offers? In a general way, we can say that an individual possesses this ability in virtue of his 'relative bargaining position'; and the obvious way to specify an individual's relative bargaining position in this context is to identify it with the extent to which he would be able to obtain preferred outcomes if everyone acted rationally (or, to put it another way, relative bargaining position refers to what an individual would secure in the 'equilibrium' outcome). The trouble is that in very many situations of interdependent decision-making, there are several plausible candidates for a principle of 'rational' choice (and, correspondingly, several plausible conceptions of 'equilibrium').

If the power of agents is to be characterised unambiguously in this way, then in each class of situations one of these candidates would have to be singled out and defended as the only acceptable one; I do not believe that this can be done at present.[7]

The difficulties which stand in the way of providing a detailed, precise and definitive characterisation of power as relative bargaining position need not trouble us further here, for all I need to do is to give a rough indication of the abilities and processes which I shall be referring to when I talk of possessing and exercising power, and to distinguish these processes from other means of getting people to do things.

I shall use the term *coercion* to refer to a subclass of the ways in which power (according to the account given above) can be exercised, namely by successfully making credible, substantial threats. For a threat to be coercive it must bring about compliance and it must do this by proposing a sanction which the recipient expects to be imposed in the event of non-compliance and which makes the non-compliant action (together with the imposition of the sanction) substantially less attractive than the compliant action (without the sanction).[8]

Offers, then, cannot be coercive. Before seeing why this is so, we must characterise the difference between offers and threats. Note first that it is not true that a threat always entails a corresponding offer and *vice versa*. When A proposes to do y if B does x, he may not specify, nor even contemplate, what he will

---

[7] An interesting attempt to do this has been made by John Charlton, who in his 'Political power' has developed this approach to power as relative bargaining position in great detail.

[8] For a fuller, more careful statement, see Robert Nozick, 'Coercion', in S. Morgenbesser, P. Suppes and M. White, eds., *Philosophy, Science and Method: Essays in Honor of Ernest Nagel* (New York: St Martin's Press, 1969); reprinted in P. Laslett, W. G. Runciman and Q. Skinner, eds., *Philosophy, Politics and Society*, Fourth Series (Oxford: Blackwell, 1972).

do if B does not do x; and (as will be clear from the following discussion of the difference between threats and offers) it is not necessarily the case that if a proposal to do y if B does x constitutes an offer, then the proposal not to do y if B does not do x is a threat.

The first obvious distinction between threats and offers is that non-compliance with the former incurs a penalty whereas compliance with the latter confers a benefit. But as a general characterisation of the difference between the two, this won't do. It could well be said that a benefit is conferred by compliance with both threats and offers, in the sense that the consequences of compliance are preferred in both cases to the consequences of non-compliance (assuming that the threatened sanction is sufficiently substantial, as it is in the case of a coercive threat). The 'benefits' and 'penalties' referred to in these two statements are being calculated from two different bases. What should the baseline be? I think Robert Nozick is on the right lines when he suggests that a proposal by A to bring about y if and only if B does x constitutes a *threat* if y makes the consequences of B's doing x worse for him than they would have been 'in the normal and expected course of events', and it constitutes an *offer* if y makes the consequences better.[9] (Obviously there will be cases where it will be difficult to say with confidence what the 'normal and expected course of events' would have been in the absence of the intervention; but this is not sufficient reason to reject this baseline.) If throffers are specified analogously, and assuming that the threatened sanction is sufficiently substantial to make compliance preferable to non-compliance, we have the picture shown in the diagram.[10]

[9] This is the heart of Nozick's distinction (in 'Coercion') between threats and offers. Of course other conditions must also be satisfied if a proposal is to count as a threat, or an offer. For example, the person making the proposal must have certain intentions, beliefs and reasons for intervening. These are dealt with by Nozick.

[10] This diagram is adapted from Hillel Steiner, 'Individual liberty', *Proceedings of the Aristotelian Society*, NS, 75 (1974–5), 33–50, at p. 39.

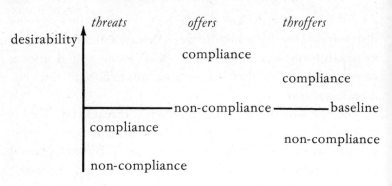

Consider the following two examples from Nozick's article on 'Coercion':

(a) P is Q's usual supplier of drugs, and today when he comes to Q he says that he will not sell them to Q, as he normally does, for $20, but rather will give them to Q if and only if Q beats up a certain person.

(b) P is a stranger who has been observing Q, and knows that Q is a drug addict. Both know that Q's usual supplier of drugs was arrested this morning and that P had nothing to do with his arrest. P approaches Q and says that he will give Q drugs if and only if Q beats up a certain person.

On Nozick's test, the intervention proposed in the first case is a throffer: it involves both a threat and an offer. The first part of the proposal is a threat because non-compliance with it (which leaves Q without drugs) makes Q worse off than he would be in the normal and expected course of events (where P supplies him with drugs in exchange for money). The second part of the proposal is an offer because in the normal and expected course of events Q does not receive drugs for beating up the person. The second case involves an offer only, since in the normal course of events P does not supply Q with drugs, nor is he expected to do so; so that obtaining drugs by complying with P's offer would be preferred by Q to the norm.

But it could be said that if in the first case P's proposal

involves a threat for the reasons Nozick gives, then 'a butcher would be threatening his customers with a penalty whenever he raised his price for meat'.[11] According to Harry Frankfurt, as long as they are not exploiting a person in a vulnerable position, both the butcher who raises his price and the drug dealer who in effect does likewise are making *offers*, albeit less attractive offers than those made before the change in price, and making poorer offers is not the same thing as making threats. Frankfurt's own proposed criteria for saying that the butcher makes a threat when he raises the price for meat are: the customer is *dependent* on the butcher for meat; the customer *needs* meat; and the butcher *exploits* the customer's dependency and need, demanding an unfair or improper price for his meat. But Frankfurt is wrong in thinking that this impairs Nozick's argument. For these three criteria amount precisely to the conditions for the proposed sanction to be a *penalty* relative to the recipient's position had the proposal not been made: if he could easily get his meat elsewhere or was indifferent about the stuff anyway, then clearly the butcher is not proposing a penalty when he increases his price, and if the price increase is not 'exploitative' but rather is more or less in line with the general run of current price increases, then compliance with the proposal does not make the customer worse off than he would have been 'in the normal and expected course of events'. In other words, Nozick's test deals satisfactorily with this case. In Nozick's own example, case (a) above, the addict does not 'in the normal and expected course of events' have to beat somebody up in exchange for his drugs and it is assumed that he cannot easily obtain his drugs elsewhere for no more than $20, so this proposal too is clearly a threat.

I said earlier that a person is *coerced* when he or she complies

[11] Harry G. Frankfurt, 'Coercion and moral responsibility', in T. Honderich, ed., *Essays on Freedom of Action* (London: Routledge and Kegan Paul, 1973).

with credible, substantial threats. It might be supposed that an *offer* can also be coercive for analogous reasons: roughly, that it secures compliance by inducing a large *difference* in utility between compliance and non-compliance. Isn't the offer made by P in Nozick's second example coercive if the addict's need is great and he cannot now obtain the drugs from anyone but P? Doesn't an employer coerce a man when he successfully offers him atrocious pay for a job without which he and his family would starve?

There are several similarities and symmetries between threats and offers, but there is also this crucial difference: it follows from the account given above of threats and offers that a rational individual would prefer not to be the recipient of a threat (whether or not he thinks he would comply) whereas he would generally be willing to have offers made to him and would not *regret* their having been made, and it is for this reason that it is inappropriate to call offers coercive.[12] This is so even if compliance with the offer involves an unfair or exploitative exchange: exploitation and injustice are not the same thing as coercion.

I conclude this discussion of power and coercion by noting that individual A's possession of power over individual B and A's ability to coerce B depend in general not only on A's possession of relevant resources but also on B's resource holdings and B's preferences and beliefs. A does not, for example, possess the ability to coerce B if B's beliefs are such that he does not find A's threat credible, or if, finding the threat credible, he is not moved by it because his preferences are such

---

[12] This view has been defended by Nozick ('Coercion', pp. 127–34 in the *Philosophy, Politics and Society* version). The only part of this book which *could* be affected by rejecting this view is a small part of the argument in Chapter 4 about community and liberty, but in fact rejecting the view in favour of the most plausible alternative position (counting successful offers which exploit persons in vulnerable positions as cases of coercion) strengthens my argument there.

that he prefers non-compliance to compliance. Clearly, then, what resources count as bases of coercion or power depends on people's preferences. In the small communities of primitive and peasant societies, every individual greatly values his reputation and the esteem in which he is held by the rest of the community; thus, the ability which the others possess (and can easily exercise) to lower his reputation through gossip and ridicule, should he engage in what they believe to be anti-social behaviour, gives them power over him (a power which, it should be noted, depends also on widely shared beliefs in the community). Again, the assistance of others at certain times is greatly valued in such communities, so that the (ever-present, tacit) throffer consisting of the offer to give aid when it is needed and the threat of withdrawing it is usually successful in getting individuals to do certain things they sometimes would not do.

A resource which can be a basis for the possession of power or of the ability to coerce is the control of and ability to use means of applying *force* or *physical constraint*. Employing force or physical constraint is itself, of course, a relatively straightforward way of getting another person to pursue a course of action he would not otherwise have pursued. I shall use either of these expressions to cover any exercise which reduces the range of actions actually open to an individual. (No other way of getting others to do things does this, as we shall see. Power, persuasion and the exercise of authority all work on the individual's will – in the case of power, by altering the incentives attached to the options; in the case of persuasion and the exercise of authority, by altering the individual's attitudes to the options – without reducing the range of options actually available to him.) The ways in which the range of available options may be reduced include restriction of the individual's movements (incarceration in a prison cell; confinement in a straitjacket); destruction, confiscation, removal, etc., of any of the necessary physical means of pursuing a course of action; and affecting the individual in such a way that he becomes literally incapable of doing certain acts (torture may do this, for example).

Another way of putting the matter is to say that when A employs force on B, B's decisions 'are irrelevant to the course of events which affect him'.[13] Force is the only way of getting people to do things they would not otherwise have done, of which it may be properly said that, because of A's actions, B *has no choice* (with respect to the excluded options).

Another process by which a person may get another to do something he would not otherwise have done is by changing his mind so that he now wants to do it, not by exercising power, but by altering his attitude to the alternative courses of action themselves and in such a way that he is aware of what is being done. This would typically be done by providing information and arguments about the nature of the choice alternatives, about the consequences of adopting different courses of action and the costs and benefits attached to them, and so on. I call this *persuasion* (although, as I have said, it doesn't matter a great deal what it is called). It roughly corresponds to what Bachrach and Baratz and others call 'influence', but this term has been used for so many different relations and processes that I am liable to be misunderstood if I use it here at all.

It might be thought that persuasion, on this account, includes the exercise of power (were it not specifically excluded), since both involve changing a person's mind so that he now *wants* to do something he didn't want to do before, by altering his attitude to the choice alternatives. But this is not so. Exercises of power in effect alter the set of alternatives facing

---

[13] Charlton, 'Political power', sec. II.

the agent, not the agent's attitude towards the (original) alternatives. For example, when A credibly threatens B with sanction s should he not perform x, B's choice is no longer between x and not-x (say), but between the conjunction of x and not-s and the conjunction of not-x and s. The threat does not cause B to see x and not-x themselves in a new light or to revise his preference between them.

Two distinct though related ways in which people are got to do things they would not otherwise have done are by means of what Talcott Parsons has called the *activation of commitments* and by means of *authority*. 'Getting someone to do something by activating a commitment', according to Brian Barry, 'is a matter of cashing in on some norm that he already has to the effect that he *ought* to act in accord with a demand from a certain source.' If, for example, an individual subscribes to a norm endowing some person with authority, then he has commitments which this person can activate. 'To take a central political example, let us say that someone has a general belief that he ought to obey the law of the country in which he lives. A new law is passed by whatever procedure constitutes the "rule of recognition" for a valid law in the country, and the person obeys it.'[14] Although this description of Barry's certainly covers the most important species of commitment-activation, I shall also include under 'activation of commitments' cashing in on norms which do *not* necessarily oblige an agent 'to act in accordance with a demand from a certain source' or give authority to some other agent. (And I shall use the concept of authority in a different way than Barry appears to be using it here.) It is perfectly possible to 'cash in' on a norm which is without an identifiable source.

That the activation of commitments and the exercise of

[14] Barry, 'Power: an economic analysis', p. 68.

authority are distinct can be seen by observing that a person may believe that he ought to obey the law of the country in which he lives and may in fact obey new laws without believing the source of the laws to be 'authoritative' (in a sense to be specified below, *or* in the sense of 'legitimate') – although his adherence to such a norm may come to be undermined as he becomes sceptical of the 'authority' of the sources of the new laws.

The method of getting people to do things which I want to call 'the exercise of *authority*' is the one which has often been singled out for special attention by Carl Friedrich, whose approach to this concept I shall follow.[15] The idea here is that A exercises authority over B when B conforms with A's communication (in the form of advice, instruction, command or whatever) because he *believes* that A *can give convincing reasons in support of it*. A need not actually give any reasons, and compliance with authority is typically obtained without specific reasons being offered. (Reasons of a general sort will usually be understood: 'it's for the sake of your health', for example.) Doctors exercise authority, in this sense, over their patients, who rarely ask for, and may be unable to understand in detail, the doctor's reasons for his advice, which is voluntarily followed because it is believed that the doctor *could* give reasons which would be found convincing.

The exercise of authority and the activation of commitments are conceptually distinct and need not be associated empirically. Often, though, authority is exercised simultaneously with the activation of commitments. An individual may subscribe to a norm requiring conformity with the instructions of the occupant of a certain role and at the same time he may view these instructions as authoritative, in the sense described above. But

---

[15] His most recent treatment is in *Tradition and Authority* (London: Macmillan, 1972).

this is not the 'authority' of which Barry speaks in the passage quoted earlier, the 'authority' which is based on legitimacy and whose exercise is one (central) way in which commitments may be activated. Two important sources of legitimacy are tradition, giving rise to 'traditional authority' which rests (to quote Max Weber) 'on an established belief in the sanctity of immemorial traditions and the legitimacy of those exercising authority under them', and 'a belief in the "legality" of enacted rules and the right of those elevated to authority under such rules to issue commands', which gives rise to what Weber called 'legal authority' (or 'legal-rational authority').[16]

It is unfortunate that 'authority' is widely used in both of these two senses – in Friedrich's sense (most commonly in speaking of 'an authority', in the sense of 'an expert') and in the sense of 'legitimate authority'. The correct interpretation or usage is not my concern here. But it is important not to confuse distinct processes. Exercising authority (according to Friedrich's account, which I am following here) is not the same thing as activating commitments. There can be (as Friedrich has stressed) legitimacy without authority and there can be authority without legitimacy.

An exercise of authority gets a person to do something he would not otherwise have done, but like persuasion (though for different reasons) he will then do it because he wants to. Authority and persuasion have this in common too: that they both (especially authority) presuppose and cannot be effective without some minimum of shared values and beliefs. They are both based on reason: persuasion works by giving a person

---

[16] Max Weber, *Economy and Society*, Vol. 1 (eds. G. Roth and C. Wittich, New York: Bedminster Press, 1968), p. 215. Weber added a 'third pure type of legitimate authority', less commonly found than legal-rational and traditional authority, which he called 'charismatic authority', 'resting on devotion to the exceptional sanctity, heroism or exemplary character of an individual person, and the normative patterns or order revealed or ordained by him'.

reasons for doing something, authority by possessing the potentiality of giving reasons.

Manipulation is commonly put on a par with force, the exercise of power and so on, as another way of getting others to do things they otherwise would not do. This is a mistake. Manipulation is the process whereby a person is got to behave or think otherwise than he would have done, in such a way that he is unaware of the source and causes of his new thought and actions (so is unaware that he has been manipulated). This does not necessarily mean that, as a result of manipulation, his thoughts and actions are not the product of rational deliberation, though (to mention two possibilities) his ability and willingness to deliberate rationally may be impaired by manipulation, and the manner in which he deliberates and his reasons for acting the way he does may themselves be wholly or in part the product of manipulation. It is not necessarily the case that a manipulated person 'has no choice' but to do what is required of him, in the sense that alternative courses of action are literally unavailable to him (for there is a difference between the unavailability of options and a manipulated choice between options). Manipulation is thus not a 'sub-concept' of force, as Bachrach and Baratz would have it. The distinguishing feature of manipulation is its *covert* nature: it is a process which is hidden from its objects. But the processes by which a person may be manipulated *include* physical constraint and the exercise of power. Manipulation, then, is not a distinct way of getting people to do things, on a par with the use of force, the exercise of power and so on.

It should be clear now (if it was not already) why it would make no sense to define anarchy as an absence of power or of authority. A society in which no individual possesses the ability to make *any* credible threat – to beat someone up, for example, or to put them to shame – is almost inconceivable (it could result only from a totally successful and bizarre form of socialisation or from genetic manipulation or neuro-surgery). So too is a society without authority, a society where nobody heeds another's advice because he believes that the other could give convincing reasons in support of it. A society without any form of coercion *is* conceivable, but even this is not entailed by statelessness, by anarchy defined as a perfect dispersion of force and a lack of political specialisation. In those societies (to be discussed in Section 1.5 below) which are the closest empirical approximations to pure anarchy, the forms of coercion and power associated with the state are replaced by *different* forms of coercion and power.

If anarchy is the absence of concentrated force and of political specialisation, it might be inferred that there is in an anarchy an approximate equality of (at least) one form of power and of coercion, namely that which is based on the ability to threaten the use of force. Even this is not the case, however, since power and the ability to coerce depend also on beliefs and values; so that an equality of control of force would entail an equality of the corresponding form of power and coercion only if the relevant beliefs and preferences were uniform throughout the community. In many anarchic communities, this uniformity might indeed be very roughly approximated. But even if it is, there is not necessarily an equality of other bases of power and coercion and hence there is not necessarily an equality of overall power or of the ability to coerce.

1.4 Community

The concept of community is central to the whole argument of this book, as the introduction to this chapter makes plain. The word is used in connection with an enormous variety of things.

Neighbourhoods, villages, towns, cities, nations and ethnic groups are all spoken of as communities; there are monastic, utopian and other 'intentional' communities; there are 'the academic community', 'the business community' and a host of other specialised communities; there is, if you please, the European Economic Community. It is clear that 'community' is an *open-textured* concept; that is to say, there is not and there cannot be an exhaustive specification of the conditions for the correct use of the concept, a set of criteria or tests which are both necessary and sufficient for something to be deemed a community.[17] There are, however, three attributes or characteristics possessed in *some* degree by *all* communities of the kinds I am concerned with in this book.

The first and most basic of these 'core' characteristics is that the set of persons who compose a community have beliefs and values in common. Communities vary greatly, of course, with respect to the range of beliefs and values shared, the degree to which these are articulated, elaborated and systematised, the strength of individuals' attachment to them, and so on. In a monastery, for example, or a 'utopian' community of the sort that flourished in the nineteenth century, there is typically an almost complete consensus on a wide range of beliefs and values, which are articulated and elaborated into a religious ideology. In many contemporary secular communes there is typically agreement on a narrower range of beliefs and values (many of them entailing a rejection of beliefs, values and practices which are dominant in the larger community) and in some cases there is a definite resistance to the creation or emergence of a shared commitment to an ideology. There are, furthermore, many other groups of people which possess some or all of the other characteristics of community to be described

[17] For the idea of an open-textured concept, see F. Waismann, *How I See Philosophy* (London: Macmillan, 1968), pp. 41–3 and 95–7. Whether or not the concept of community is 'essentially contestable' (a concept which is currently receiving too much attention from political theorists) is in my view not worth discussing.

shortly and whose members share strongly held beliefs and values but do not elaborate them into ideologies, myths or religions (of which beliefs and values are of course constituent elements). Accordingly (and bearing in mind the argument that 'community' is an open-textured concept) it would be altogether too restrictive to require (as Carl Friedrich does)[18] that, if a group of people is to be deemed a community, its members must have in common not only beliefs and values but also ideologies, myths and religions.

(It is tempting to treat *communication* (the total amount of communication, or the relative density of communication channels, or the members' capacity for communication with each other, or some such) as a second universal characteristic of community – to say that between the members of a community there is communication and that the boundaries of a community are marked by a relative decline in the frequency of communication. Karl Deutsch has in fact *defined* community in this way (in his *Nationalism and Social Communication* and elsewhere). But it is clear that this characteristic and that of shared beliefs and values are so much interdependent that there is little point in including both of them as criteria for community; and of the two it is the possession of shared beliefs and values which is the more fundamental, for communication is made possible by it and is generally (though not always) a consequence of it, whereas it is less generally true that communication promotes a convergence of beliefs and values.)

The second characteristic of community is that relations between members should be *direct* and they should be *many-sided*. Relations are direct to the extent that they are unmediated – by representatives, leaders, bureaucrats, institutions such as

[18] Carl Friedrich (in *Man and His Government*, New York: McGraw-Hill, 1963, at p. 144) stipulatively defines a community as 'a togetherness of persons who are united by having in common some of their values, interests, ideas (including ideologies), myths, utopias and their symbols, as well as religion and its rituals'.

those of the state, or by codes, abstractions and reifications (about which more later). A collection of individuals might share a wide range of strongly-held beliefs and values, yet live in considerable isolation from each other, pursuing common ends not by dealing directly with each other but through the agency of the state (as do many so-called local communities) or by appealing to some formal code or ideology or an abstract conception of the community itself (as in many of the utopian communities, where relations between individuals may be closely regulated). It seems to me that we should want to say that, other things being equal, a group of individuals amongst whom relations are to some extent mediated is to that extent less of a community than a group in which relations are relatively direct.

Similarly, we should want to say that, other things being equal, a group of individuals whose relations are many-sided is more of a community than one in which relations are specialised, narrowly confined to one area. The 'academic community' is indeed a community, for its members share certain beliefs and values in common and there is even (a very limited amount of) cooperation amongst them (this is the third characteristic of community, to be discussed below), but relations amongst its members (in their roles as academics) are limited and it is accordingly less of a community than, for example, primitive communities and most contemporary communes, whose members relate to each other through more aspects or facets of themselves.

The third and final characteristic of community is that of *reciprocity*. I shall use this term to cover a range of arrangements and relations and exchanges, including mutual aid, some forms of cooperation and some forms of sharing. Each individual act in a system of reciprocity is *usually* characterised by a combination of what one might call short-term altruism and long-term self-interest: I help you out now in the (possibly vague, uncertain and uncalculating) expectation that you will help me out in the future. Reciprocity is made up of a series of acts each of which is short-run altruistic (benefiting others at a cost to the altruist) but which together *typically* make every participant better off. What I am calling reciprocity can be usefully located on a segment of the continuum of reciprocity forms proposed by Marshall Sahlins in his account of transactions in primitive societies.[19] The end-points of Sahlins' spectrum are 'generalised reciprocity' and 'negative reciprocity' and the mid-point is 'balanced reciprocity'.

In *generalised reciprocity*, the transactions are 'putatively altruistic', the obligation to reciprocate is vague and diffuse, and the altruism is not conditional upon reciprocation. There can be sustained one-way flows, if the recipient is in a difficult position. 'The material side of the transaction is repressed by the social.' Nevertheless, the altruism involved here *is* normally reciprocated. In this category, Sahlins mentions sharing, hospitality, help and generosity.

In *balanced reciprocity*, there is direct exchange. Normally, the exchange is of goods which are of roughly commensurate utility and reciprocation must be made upon or shortly after receipt. In perfectly balanced reciprocity, the exchange is simultaneous and involves the same type of goods in the same amounts. The transactions on both sides of balanced reciprocity are *conditional*: one-way flows are not tolerated and 'the relations between people are disrupted by a failure to reciprocate within limited time and equivalence leeways'.

Negative reciprocity is 'the attempt to get something for nothing with impunity' and includes 'haggling', 'barter', 'gambling', 'chicanery' and 'theft'. Each party here is out for the 'unearned increment' at the other's expense. Reciprocation, says Sahlins, is again conditional, though it is not conditional in

[19] Marshall Sahlins, *Stone Age Economics* (London: Tavistock, 1974), ch. 5.

the sense in which balanced reciprocity is; the flow may of course be one-way, when the 'recipient' (victim) is unable or unwilling to reciprocate.

The range of practices I shall refer to simply as reciprocity corresponds to the segment of Sahlins' spectrum lying between balanced reciprocity and generalised reciprocity, including the latter pole but not the former. Straightforward balanced reciprocity or direct exchange is of course found in most communities but is not a distinguishing characteristic of community. At the generalised pole of the range of reciprocity practices is giving (food, labour, the loan of tools, or whatever) which is not conditional on reciprocation, even though in practice there usually is reciprocation. The reciprocity which is practised in the communities I shall be using as examples in the next two chapters is generally less pure than this, though not far from the generalised pole. (A series of exchanges which are unbalanced on the side of generalised reciprocity may tend to build trust and push the exchange further towards the generalised pole.)[20] In typical reciprocity the individual expects that his gift or assistance will be repaid; sometimes the expectation is vague and uncalculating, sometimes it must be somewhat less so, as when the primitive or peasant cultivator gives up time to help others harvest crops quickly in the firm expectation that those he has helped will do the same for him. If continued giving goes unreciprocated, it will usually be terminated, except where the recipient is needy or unable to reciprocate.

It is worth noting here that *fraternity*, rarely used now as a synonym for community, consists essentially of the practice of generalised reciprocity in certain contexts – the 'solidarity' between workers during strikes or following a pit disaster, for example.[21]

There is much talk, among both admirers and detractors of

[20] Compare Sahlins, *Stone Age Economics*, p. 223.

community, of communitarian relations being 'loving' or 'emotional' or 'intense'. If it were stipulatively required of 'community' that a person's relations with most or many of the other members of the community were of this sort, then very few communities would qualify and those which did would be found to be short-lived. Relations of this kind are generally about as confined in communities as they are outside them, in many cases more so. It is *friendship*, rather than love, which is more extensive in many communities, and it is friendship rather than love which is an important goal, perhaps the central goal, for many of the individuals who form or join modern, secular communes. By friendship, I mean something more than what is commonly meant by this term; I have in mind something like the notion of friendship elaborated by Aristotle in the *Nicomachean Ethics* and used by Abrams and McCulloch in their study of contemporary communes.[22] In the words of Abrams and McCulloch, 'the defining properties of friendship are intimacy ("a friend is a second self") and activity – doing something together, not just being together'. It involves mutual concern, and although 'the reciprocity of friendship means that one gets back what one gives', there is no calculation of benefits and costs. It requires an approximate equality and strong, secure selves. 'To be capable of friendship one must first know and esteem oneself. Then one must engage on terms of equality in an active relationship through the enacting of which one experiences the goodness of others while demonstrating goodness to them.' Friendship is therefore a precarious project, not often fully successful. It would be too strong a criterion for 'community' and will not be part of my characterisation of the

---

[21] Compare Eric Hobsbawm, 'The idea of fraternity', *New Society*, 34 (Nov. 1975): 'Fraternity is, at bottom, a certain type of social co-operation. . . . a relation between a group of equals for the utmost mutual help and aid . . .'

[22] Philip Abrams and Andrew McCulloch, *Communes, Sociology and Society* (Cambridge: Cambridge University Press, 1976). See especially ch. 2.

concept. Nevertheless, community *can* make wide friendship possible, because in a community relations are direct and many-sided and reciprocity is practised, and these things facilitate the development of friendship.

There is, finally, a condition which, like friendship, is too strong a criterion for 'community' but often appears, in a central place, in accounts of that concept. Martin Buber is referring to it when he writes of 'the need of man to feel his own house as a room in some greater, all-embracing structure in which he is at home, to feel that the other inhabitants of it with whom he lives and works are all acknowledging and confirming his individual existence'.[23] What we have here is a condition of 'transcendence' combined with a sense of belonging and mutual affirmation. This combination is indeed found in some communities and it is, like friendship, an important aspiration of many people who form and join contemporary communes. But it is not found in all communities (as I have characterised them above) and as a goal of intentional communities it is not often achieved.

If community is characterised by shared values and beliefs, direct and many-sided relations, and the practice of reciprocity, then it is clear that communities must be relatively small and stable. In a large and changing mass of people, few relations between individuals can be direct or many-sided, and reciprocity cannot flourish on a wide scale, since its continuation for any length of time requires *some* actual reciprocation, which in turn requires stable relations with known individuals. Of course, each of the criteria of community in my account is not an all-or-nothing test but can be satisfied in varying degrees, so that a collection of individuals may be more or less of a community. Thus, when I say that a community must be relatively small and stable, I mean that each of the three characteristics must

[23] Martin Buber, *Paths in Utopia* (Boston: Beacon Press, 1958), p. 140.

become diluted or attenuated or restricted as size increases and to that degree there is less community.

1.5 Anarchic communities

During almost all of the time since *Homo sapiens* emerged, he has lived in stateless 'primitive' communities. These primitive anarchies fall into three groups. There is firstly a fairly well-defined division between what I shall call *acephalous* societies and those with systems of *centralised redistribution*; and secondly a subdivision of the redistributive systems into *chiefdoms* and *big-man systems*. Almost all the societies of hunters and gatherers were acephalous bands (well-known exceptions are the Indians of the Northwest American coast); so were many tribal societies. In some of these acephalous societies, chiefdoms gradually arose. (The development of chiefdoms into states will be briefly reviewed in Section 3.3.)

In the acephalous societies there is only the minimum concentration of force and scarcely any political specialisation at all. There is at most the occasional, *ad hoc* concentration of force in the hands of the 'warriors' when fighting outsiders and in the hands of the 'vengeance groups' pursuing 'self-help justice'. In many hunting and gathering bands even this concentration is rare, since violence of these kinds occurs infrequently. The division of political labour in acephalous societies is similarly undeveloped. There are no leadership positions with formal status. There are individuals with prestige and authority (in the sense specified in Section 1.3), but their advice and recommendations cannot be backed by force or power. Their prestige and authority is based on personal qualities. If a man acquires a reputation as a successful hunter or skilled mediator, he is respected and his advice is heeded – but only in the matter of hunting or dispute settlement. Occasionally an individual combines several excellences and may become something of a charismatic leader, but only so long as he continues to be respected and therefore only so long as he performs well. The only widespread exception to this pattern is that males usually have greater prestige than females and elders are accorded greater respect and their advice followed. There are also particular exceptions to this pattern of approximate equality of political participation: for example, in the acephalous tribes of the Nuer there is a position known as the 'leopard-skin chief' (though not a chief at all) whose occupant mediates in disputes; but he has no power and controls no concentrated force, so cannot enforce his decisions, and when not mediating he lives the same sort of life as other adult Nuer males.

The redistributive systems are in the first place characterised by a 'centralisation of reciprocities' (to be discussed more fully in Section 3.2). Chiefdoms have hierarchies of formal, hereditary status, with strong theocratic and divinely sanctioned leadership. The chief or big-man collects dues – a levy on the produce of the community – and is under obligation to use them generously for the benefit of his people. In addition to channelling the redistribution of produce, the chief organises religious ceremonies, festivities, war, public building works and so on. So there is in a chiefdom considerable inequality of prestige and authority and some inequality of participation. Nevertheless, a chief has no more power, in the sense I have been using this word, than other individuals, and he has no control of concentrated force. His prestige is in large measure dependent on his generosity. In the big-man systems, the big-man at first attracts followers because he possesses qualities of the sort that make charismatic leaders in acephalous societies, and then builds and maintains a position of leadership through generous giving, a position with greater prestige than that of leaders in acephalous societies. Not only does the big-man, like the chief, lack power and the control of concentrated force, but his position tends to be more personal, less formally established, and hence less stable than that of the chief.

On my account of 'anarchy', then, big-man systems and chiefdoms, as well as acephalous societies, are anarchies, with the acephalous societies approaching much more closely to the pure anarchy pole than the redistributive systems. In all three, there is only a limited concentration of force and crucially there is no means of enforcing collective decisions, even in the chiefdoms with their greater division of political labour.

These primitive societies constitute the principal historical examples of anarchies. But I intend to draw also on the experience of certain other kinds of communities which are not strictly speaking anarchies. The first of these is the peasant community. Far from being stateless, peasant communities are distinguished from primitive tribal societies of cultivators (with which they nevertheless have much in common) above all by their integration into a larger society with a state. The peasant shares with the primitive tribal cultivator many of the features of the 'domestic mode of production' (which I shall describe in some detail in Section 3.2) but unlike the latter he must produce a fund of rent, to be paid in produce, labour or money to people outside his community who control concentrated force and thereby wield power over him.[24] Nevertheless, the local community in *some* peasant societies is *internally* quasi-anarchic, for the community in these societies is largely responsible for the maintenance of internal order and the settlement of disputes between its members and in some cases for maintaining an approximate equality, and it may discharge these functions with considerable autonomy from lord and state. 'The village community', writes Shanin, 'operates to a considerable extent as an autonomous society', but 'the sep-

---

[24] See, for example, Eric R. Wolf, *Peasants* (Englewood Cliffs, NJ: Prentice-Hall, 1966), ch. 1.

arateness of the village is generally broken in at least two ways. Firstly, there are always some relations between different villages . . . Secondly, there are the more or less centralised networks of domination which penetrate the countryside, linking political and cultural hegemony with exploitation by landlords, state and town.'[25]

Because many peasant communities are internally quasi-anarchic, we should expect to find, and do find (see Sections 2.4 and 3.2), that the means by which they maintain social order and the means of containing the development of inequality are similar to some of those found in the primitive stateless societies. Since, as I shall argue in the following two chapters, these alternative social control mechanisms can work in anarchies only where there is community, we should expect to find, and do find, that it is in precisely the peasant quasi-anarchies most closely resembling true communities – the so-called 'closed corporate peasant communities' – that these social controls are most developed and effective.

The closed corporate peasant community maintains a well-defined and relatively impermeable boundary between itself and the rest of the world, takes a strict and narrow view of membership, restricting participation of the non-members in the running of the community and their ownership of land, and exercises partial control over the disposition of land, preventing its sale to outsiders where it is privately owned and redistributing it periodically among its members where it is owned in common. Closed corporate communities can still be found in Central America and the Andes and in parts of Asia; before the present century they were common over much of East and West Europe.[26]

The final group of historical examples I shall draw on are the

[25] Teodor Shanin, 'The nature and logic of the peasant economy', Part I, *Journal of Peasant Studies*, 1 (1973), 63–80.
[26] See, for example, Eric R. Wolf, 'Types of Latin American peasantry: a

so-called 'intentional communities'. Like peasant communities, they are located in societies with states. But many of them, again like many of the peasant communities, are internally quasi-anarchic, making collective decisions and settling disputes without recourse to the state. Some of them are, by choice or by necessity, economically nearly self-sufficient as well. Indeed, these communities are commonly an attempt to construct an entire way of life alternative to that of the society from which they partially withdraw. There is great variation in the degree of division of political labour, and I shall be especially interested in those intentional communities in which this is at a minimum (as it usually is in the 'secular family commune' – the dominant form in the wave of commune activity which began in the 1960s and is still continuing) and in comparing such communities with the 'utopian communities' which flourished especially in America and England in the nineteenth century and which were more politically centralised, with a religious or political ideology and a strong charismatic leadership. In referring to intentional communities in the remainder of the book I shall have in mind chiefly the various American and English utopian communities and communes of the nineteenth and twentieth centuries, though brief reference will also be made to the Israeli *kibbutzim* and *shitufim*.

One category of putative internal anarchies which do *not* provide very useful information relevant to the arguments in this book are the communities and collectives set up by anarchists themselves in revolutionary situations, most notably

preliminary discussion', *American Anthropologist*, 57 (1955), 452–71; 'Closed corporate peasant communities in Mesoamerica and Central Java', *Southwestern Journal of Anthropology*, 13 (1957), 1–18; *Peasants*, ch. 3; Jerome Blum, 'The European village as community: origins and functions', *Agricultural History*, 45 (1971), 157–78; 'The internal structure and polity of the European village community from the fifteenth to the nineteenth century', *Journal of Modern History*, 43 (1971), 541–76; Samuel L. Popkin, *The Rational Peasant* (Berkeley: University of California Press, 1979), chs. 1–3.

those agrarian collectives of the Spanish Revolution which best approximated total communities. The problem with these is that, apart from being short-lived (as indeed were some of the intentional communities referred to in the last paragraph), they were made possible by and existed precariously in most unusual circumstances, so that they cannot be reliably used as a basis for generalisations about such things as the maintenance of stateless social order or the compatibility of community and liberty.

I have been referring to these empirical instances of anarchy and quasi-anarchy as *communities*, and in fact it is the case that, by the criteria of 'community' given earlier, these anarchies *are* in varying degrees also communities. Their members hold in common a wide range of values and beliefs; relations between them are generally direct and many-sided; and they practise reciprocity in many areas. These criteria for community are satisfied more imperfectly in precisely those cases which are less purely anarchic: in the big-man systems and chiefdoms, where a division of political labour has begun to develop, relations are to that extent mediated and reciprocity centralised; in the peasant communities some relations and some of the functions of reciprocity are mediated by the external holders of power to the extent that these control, extract resources from, and otherwise intervene in the community; and the same is true of intentional communities in inverse proportion as their internal relations are mediated by strong leadership and by religious and other ideologies.

My reliance in the bulk of the book on 'primitive', peasant and intentional communities will no doubt draw charges of irrelevance, utopianism or romanticism. But I do not see how anyone interested in anarchy or in community can or ought to avoid examining these communities, for they constitute the chief, almost the only historical examples of anarchy and quasi-anarchy and they are important examples of community on almost any account of that concept.

2

Social order without the state

My point of departure for the main argument to be developed in this book is that, in *any sort of society*, social order is generally found desirable, but its maintenance is nevertheless problematical and the chief immediate sources of the problem are to do with social order being an example of what economists call a *public* or *collective* good and with individual preferences having certain characteristics. I shall explain and provide a partial defence of this starting point in the following section.

When I say that the maintenance of social order is a problem, I mean roughly that it is not ensured merely by socialisation reinforced by ritual and the gestures and signs of everyday conversation and other social intercourse (important though these are), but requires in addition the use of controls which involve the use of threats. In this sense, the maintenance of social order is a problem which is not peculiar to possessive market societies; it is also a problem (though perhaps a less acute one) for primitive societies without markets and with individual possession of only the barest 'non-strategic' goods; and even in the sort of society envisaged by certain utopian socialist and communitarian anarchist writers it would not be solved as effortlessly as they generally suppose.

2.1 Social order and public goods

Before embarking on the argument about the maintenance of social order, a brief account of the concept of a public good is required.

A good is said to be *public* if it is characterised by some degree of *indivisibility* or *jointness of supply* (with respect to a given public), that is, if consumption of any unit of the good by any member of the public in question does not prevent any other member of the public consuming the same unit, or if, equivalently, any unit of the good, once produced, can be made available to every member of the public.[1] Clearly, there are degrees of indivisibility. The good may be only partially available to some individuals and in varying degrees; and actual consumption of the good may vary between individuals. If every individual's actual consumption of any given unit is the same, then the good is said to be *perfectly* indivisible. This does not imply that every individual's *utility* in consuming the good is the same. An example of a good which approximates fairly closely to perfect indivisibility is clean air (for publics in areas in which the air is uniformly clean). National defence is a standard example of a jointly supplied good, but it is perhaps less than perfectly indivisible (and possibly not viewed as a good at all by every member of the nation). A perfectly *divisible* good, on the other hand, is one which can be divided between individuals, and once any part of it has been appropriated by an individual, the same part cannot simultaneously be made available to others. Such a good is called a *private good*. A private good is thus a polar case, and any good which is not a pure private good is in some degree public. It is clear, then, that a great many goods have *some* element of publicness.

Private goods and public goods are often inseparable; it is not possible to provide the public good without also providing a private good, and conversely. I have cited the standard example of national defence as an imperfect public good: in fact it can be decomposed (analytically at least) into deterrence, which is a pure public good, and protection from attack, which is an

---

[1] On public goods, see my *Anarchy and Cooperation* (London and New York: Wiley, 1976), ch. 2, and the works cited there.

impure public good (i.e. is imperfectly indivisible), and of course the expenditures necessary to create national defence also produce private goods for the shareholders and employees of business firms.[2]

A good may exhibit indivisibility or jointness of supply and yet be such that it is possible to prevent particular individuals from consuming it. A road or bridge or park is such a good. Once supplied to one individual, it *can* be made available to others but it need not be, for particular individuals can be excluded. If this is not possible, the good is said to exhibit *non-excludability*. Clearly, if a good is non-excludable it is not possible to make an individual pay for consuming or using it, as it is in the case of roads, bridges and parks, for which tolls and admission charges can be imposed on users. Some indivisible goods are necessarily non-excludable; it is simply not possible to exclude particular individuals from consuming them. This is more or less true of clean air and many other environmental public goods. But many indivisible goods can be supplied in either the excludable mode or the non-excludable.

For some goods which have been cited in the past as instances of non-excludable goods, it has been claimed that a closer inspection would show that they *can* be provided in the excludable mode (though often at an 'uneconomic' cost) or that they can be decomposed into several component goods some of which are divisible or, though indivisible, are excludable. Generally speaking in these cases, if excludable provision of the good is to be brought about, there has to be a redefinition of existing property rights or creation of individual property rights where none existed before, as well as technological innovation.[3] This argument has been made in connection with

[2] Cf. William Loehr and Todd Sandler, eds., *Public Goods and Public Policy* (Beverley Hills: Sage, 1978), p. 23 and ch. 6.
[3] For some illustrations see David Friedman, *The Machinery of Freedom: Guide to a Radical Capitalism* (New York: Harper and Row, 1973), for example in ch. 15 ('Sell the streets').

social order and I shall have more to say about it later in this section and in Section 2.3 which examines the claim that social order can be satisfactorily provided by private firms competing in the open market. It is true that it is usually taken for granted that social order is a non-excludable public good,[4] and it does indeed turn out that some of the component goods which make up 'social order' are very imperfectly indivisible and can be provided in the excludable mode. Nevertheless, as I shall argue below, there remains an important element of publicness.

If a good is both indivisible and non-excludable, it is possible for an individual to be a 'free rider', that is, to consume or benefit from the good without contribution to its production costs. More precisely, if some of the good is already in supply, then an individual may be a free rider only if the good exhibits some degree of indivisibility *and* the individual in question is not in fact excluded from consumption, whether he contributes or not; and if the good is not yet provided in any amount, then an individual can *expect* to be able to take a free ride only if the good will be jointly supplied *and* he expects that he will not be excluded. If exclusion is actually impossible, this second condition obviously obtains; but it may also obtain even when the good is to be excludable.

Under certain conditions (to be discussed below) an individual may decide to attempt to be a free rider, making no contribution to the cost of providing a public good in the hope of benefiting from others' contributions. If every member of the public so decides, the public good will not be provided at all. Non-contribution would be the rational course of action for an egoist (one who considers only his own costs and benefits) if the costs to him of making any contribution exceed the benefits *to him* of the additional amount of the public good which could be provided out of his contribution.

[4] As I did in *Anarchy and Cooperation*.

Relatively straightforward and important instances of public goods and the free rider problem are to be found in connection with problems of resources and the environment. Consider for example a polluted lake, a receptacle for sewage and industrial wastes. Let us assume that an improvement in the quality of the water in the lake is considered to be a good by all the owners of houses and factories on its shore, who like to swim in it, sail on it, use it in their industrial processes, and so on, if it is sufficiently clean. If the water is well-circulated around the lake, such an improvement would be a public good for this group of people; it would be both indivisible (tending to perfect indivisibility with increasingly thorough circulation) and non-excludable (assuming that particular individuals cannot be or are not in fact excluded from using the lake). A lakeshore dweller or factory-owner could contribute to an improvement in water quality by taking his wastes elsewhere, treating them before discharging them into the lake or modifying his product. Making such a contribution to the public good is costly, and each member of the public good would most prefer everyone else to make a contribution while he has a free ride; but he would prefer everyone to contribute, including himself, to nobody doing anything about the polluted lake. Despite everyone having a common interest in a cleaner lake, nobody would voluntarily contribute to improving it if the costs of his doing so would exceed the benefits *to him* of the improvement in the water's quality which would result from *his* contribution.

Most, if not all, jointly supplied goods are characterised by a certain degree of *rivalness*. A good is said to be *rival* to the extent that the *consumption* of a unit of the good by one individual affects the benefits to others who *consume* the same unit. In the polar case of a private good, the consumption of a particular unit prevents any other individual from consuming it at all, and it is said to be *perfectly rival*. Such public facilities as parks, beaches, roads and 'wilderness' areas are examples of goods with some degree of rivalness: beyond a certain level of use, an individual's utility from consumption is lowered as a result of consumption by others.

Related to, but distinct from publicness is the phenomenon of *externality* or external effect. On the widest definition, an externality is said to be present whenever an individual's utility is affected by an activity of some other individual. On this account, most activities exert some sort of externality. A more restrictive definition stipulates that the interdependence between the two individuals must be 'untraded', that is to say, the individual affected by the externality is not compensated for the harm done him in the case of a negative externality and does not pay for the benefit accruing to him in the case of a positive externality. On either the wider or the more restrictive account of 'externality', the production of a non-excludable indivisible good produces external effects, but externalities are involved in interactions other than those associated with the production or consumption of public goods.

I asserted at the outset that social order is a public good. This assertion must now be amplified and defended.

In the most restrictive of its common usages, 'social order' refers to an absence, more or less complete, of violence, a state of affairs in which people are relatively safe from physical attack.

On a somewhat broader view, 'social order' is security of property (against theft and damage at the hands of other individuals) as well as of persons. This is the order Hobbes was concerned with and he called it Peace. 'Property' is here a shorthand for a variety of entitlements or use-rights. These range from property in the narrow modern sense of lawful, exclusive, individual ownership backed ultimately by the force of the state to the more conditional and non-exclusive usufructs sanctioned by the community in primitive societies. The point in both cases is that the individual or household has an entitlement, sanctioned by the community at large or by the state, to control and use the resources in question. In primitive societies ownership of important resources, especially land, is formally vested in chiefs, clans, lineages, bands or a kin-based collective core of the living group, but the households have access to the resources and day to day control over their use – conditional entitlements which in tribal societies can be over-ridden by the chief or the lineage of which they are a part.[5]

It is widely assumed that social order, viewed as security of persons and their property, is a good and furthermore that it is a public good. That it is a *good* (i.e. is desired) is widely taken for granted because life *without* it is acknowledged to be undesirable. For a strong statement there is the famous passage in Chapter 13 of *Leviathan* where the state of nature, 'wherein men live without other security, than what their own strength, and their own invention shall furnish them withall', is described by Hobbes as a condition in which

there is no place for Industry; because the fruit thereof is uncertain: and consequently no Culture of the Earth; no Navigation, nor use of the commodities that may be imported by Sea; no commodious Building; no Instruments of moving, and removing such things as require much force; no Knowledge of the face of the Earth; no account of Time; no Arts; no Letters; no Society; and which is worst of all, continuall feare, and danger of violent death; And the life of man, solitary, poore, nasty, brutish, and short.

Without necessarily agreeing with the details of this picture, we can agree that, because it is a precondition of the pursuit and attainment of a variety of desired ends, security of person and property is generally found attractive (to put it no more strongly). But this conclusion needs to be qualified and tightened

[5] See Sahlins, *Stone Age Economics*, especially pp. 92–3. For a detailed hunting–gathering example, see Richard Borshay Lee, *The !Kung San: Men, Women, and Work in a Foraging Society* (Cambridge: Cambridge University Press, 1979), especially pp. 118–19, 334–9, 360–1.

up. There seems little doubt that almost everyone prefers more security of person and property to less, at least if everything else remains the same, that is to say, if he can enjoy without cost greater security without others doing so. In this sense, security is clearly a good. Of course, an individual can enjoy greater security without others doing so only if security can be provided as a *private* good – as indeed it can, to some extent, in the form of bodyguards and other forms of individual protection having no or negligible side effects on the security of others. But it cannot be inferred from an individual's preference for security for himself that he has a preference for greater security for everyone. This applies to any individual *ceteris paribus* preferences. An individual may want to be the owner of a car, other things being equal; but this does not imply that he prefers everyone owning a car to nobody owning one, since universal ownership brings with it costs to the individual (in the form of danger, pollution, and so on) as well as the assumed benefits of his owning a car, and these must be set against the benefits of safety, health, peace and quiet of universal non-ownership (as well as the costs of his not owning a car). Similarly, a preference for greater wealth rather than less, other things being equal, does not imply a desire for greater wealth if others are to have greater wealth as well. Again, this is so, even if we disregard envy and other ways in which the individual's utility depends on comparisons between others' wealth and his own, because there may (in the view of the individual) be costs associated with living in a generally wealthier society which are absent in a poorer one.[6]

Security of person and property can, as I have said, be provided as a private good and so enjoyed exclusively by a single individual. But there are a wider range of ways in which it can be provided as an indivisible and non-excludable good, for

---

[6] Cf. Brian Barry, *The Liberal Theory of Justice* (Oxford: Clarendon Press, 1973), ch. 11.

example in the form of police, law courts, and so on, operating so as to enhance the security of every individual's person and property. In this case (and in the case of any non-excludable indivisible good), an individual's *ceteris paribus* preference for more rather than less is of a hypothetical nature; he cannot have more security (or cleaner water in his lake or cleaner air over his city) without others having more also. He may or may not prefer an increased provision of security in these circumstances. He may *not* desire such security because, say, he is a member of a society with unequally distributed property who has little property to protect and who expects to benefit from a free-for-all and to be able to defend his gains, and because the security in question – which in any case would generally be far from perfectly indivisible – affords him much less protection than many others enjoy. ('The empirical data . . . make it abundantly clear that the poor do not receive the same treatment at the hands of the agents of law-enforcement as the well-to-do or middle class. This differential treatment is systematic and complete.')[7] For such a person, who would want security for himself *only if* it were denied (some) others, it is not clear that non-excludable, indivisible security is to be reckoned a good at all. We might say that when he can get it privately, it is a good; but when it can only be had publicly, it is for him a bad. If it is indeed the case that, while some people have the Hobbesian preference for security of person and property over the 'state of nature', there are others who, for whatever reason, have the opposite preference, then it could be (and has been) argued that the likely upshot is that security is maintained and enforced unilaterally by those who benefit from it. It could also be argued that this asymmetric social order is just the sort of order which is in fact maintained by modern states; and some

[7] William J. Chambliss and Robert B. Seidman, *Law, Order and Power* (Reading, Mass.: Addison-Wesley, 1971), p. 475.

(Marxist) writers would argue that this is necessarily so, that this is a central part of what the state *is*.

Whatever the truth of these arguments, it is surely the case that a sufficiently symmetric security would be preferred by everyone to insecurity; that there is a security of person and property which is desired by all. Thus, that part of social order (viewed as security of person and property) which cannot be provided in the form of private goods – and I shall argue in Section 2.3 that there is such a part – is a public *good*. This is true *a fortiori* of the more restricted conception of social order as safety from physical attack, or security of persons.

There are two other, much broader, common conceptions of social order. According to the first of these, social order lies in the day-to-day *predictability* of social life. There is social order, on this account, to the extent that most of the time people do not have their expectations upset – they do not venture unwarned onto the (English) road one morning to discover that everyone is driving on the right-hand side, for example. For most of the people most of the time the existence of this kind of order is convenient or comforting. But it is not itself a public good; only parts of it are public goods, or rather, the production of certain public goods contributes to it. Security of person and property, for example, would presumably be a part of social order in this broader sense, and as we have seen this is typically a public good. Consider, however, the almost universal practice of driving on the left in Great Britain. This too contributes to social order in the broad sense, but no public good is involved. It is a *convention*, a solution to a coordination problem, and once a convention is established there is no incentive for any participant to deviate from conformity to it.[8] An individual

---

[8] See David Lewis, *Convention: A Philosophical Study* (Cambridge, Mass.: Harvard University Press, 1969).

benefits from the provision of a public good *whether or not* he contributes, but this is plainly not so in the case of a convention; there is little satisfaction to be had in driving on the right when others are driving on the left. A second reason why social order in the sense of predictability is not a public good is that while much of this order depends on general conformity to established norms, customs, conventions and other regularities, some of a particular individual's day-to-day expectations may be based on established relations with specific others which may be neither customary, conventional or normal in the wider society nor productive of a public good even for the individuals involved.

According to the second broad conception of social order, it consists of a general conformity to social norms. Social order on this account is not a public good, though again the production of certain public goods contributes to it. And this is so, whether we think of norms as regularities in behaviour or action, or as prescriptions or standards, or as a combination of these. I prefer the last of these approaches, according to which a social norm is a prescription or standard with which most people actually comply. Plainly, this account of social order as general conformity with norms has much in common with the preceding account, for a degree of conformity to norms conduces to, indeed is a condition of, the day-to-day predictability of social life, and it encompasses the two narrow accounts of social order, provided that the norms to which there is to be conformity include prescriptions against assaults on persons and their property. Conformity to these two norms, and to many others which would presumably be included in those to which conformity is required for social order, contributes to the production of a public good (with the qualifications noted earlier). But there are many norms, conformity to which does not contribute to the production of a public good. These include conventions, which if they are solutions to pure coordination problems, emerge 'spontaneously' and do not need to be maintained by any sort of controls, because there is no incentive for any participant to deviate from them (as there is for a rational egoist to deviate from agreement to contribute to the provision of public goods – that is, to be a free rider).[9]

My concern here is with social order of a kind which is thought desirable by most people in any society but which at the same time is not maintained without controls of one sort or another. This is true of any form of social order which is a public good. It is thus true, with certain qualifications, of the narrow conceptions of social order as security of persons and their property. It is social order in these senses which I shall have chiefly in mind in the following discussion of social control.[10] But, as we have seen, there are public goods elements in social order viewed either as predictability or as conformity to norms, and most of what I shall have to say about social control applies to the production of these public goods. It applies also to the production of public goods not involved in social order.

Now insofar as social order is a (non-excludable) public good, there is a problem, as we have seen, about its provision. Because an individual benefits when a public good is provided whether or not he has made any contribution to its provision, he would most prefer everyone *else* to provide it. Under certain conditions, the result is that the public good is not provided at all or a less than optimal amount is provided (that is, everyone would prefer a larger amount to be provided). This, as Mancur Olson has argued in his well-known study of *The Logic of Collective Action*,[11] is more likely to happen in larger publics than

---

[9] See Lewis, *Convention*.
[10] I shall use the term 'social control' in the correspondingly narrow sense according to which it refers only to the production of behaviour which contributes to this sort of social order.

in smaller ones. The chief reason for this is that the larger the public, the smaller the benefit which accrues to any individual member from the additional amount of the public good provided out of his contribution, so that in a relatively large group this benefit is likely to be exceeded by the cost to him of making the contribution, whereas in a relatively small group this is less likely to be the case. A further reason is that the difficulty and costs of organising the provision of the public good are likely to increase with the size of the group. The large group will provide itself with the public good only if there is a *selective* incentive for an individual to contribute, a private benefit which the individual can enjoy *only if* he contributes. Thus, a trade union is primarily formed in order to provide for its members certain public goods, such as higher wages and better working conditions. But no individual, though he desires such things, would pay his dues; he would hope to be a 'free rider'. Hence the 'closed shop' is operated (employment is conditional upon membership), members enjoy sickness benefits, and so on. These things are selective benefits. The respect and approval of one's community for contributing to a public good by refraining from violence, for example, is also a selective incentive.

Olson's conclusion is broadly correct, but partly for reasons which do not appear in his argument. In the first place, the relation between the size of the public and the amount of the public good its members will provide for themselves in the absence of selective incentives is somewhat more complicated than Olson supposed. In particular, the extent of an individual's contribution to the provision of a public good depends not only on the size of the public but also on the individual's utility function (which tells us how much of a *numéraire* private good he is willing to sacrifice for a given increase in the supply of the public good) and on the transformation function (which

[11] Cambridge, Mass.: Harvard University Press, 1965.

specifies the quantity of the public good which can be produced with a given input of the private good) and on the degrees of divisibility and of rivalness of the public good.[12]

The second problem with Olson's analysis of public goods provision is that it is entirely static. Its conclusions about public goods provision are derived from assumptions about individual preferences at one point in time. Individuals are supposed, in effect, to make only one choice, once and for all, about how much to contribute to the provision of the public good. Time plays no part in the analysis. Plainly, with respect to most public goods, the choice of whether or not to contribute and how much to contribute is a recurring choice and in some cases it is a choice which is permanently before the individual. This is certainly true of the individual's choice of whether or not to act peaceably, to refrain from violence, robbery and fraud, and so on. However, although a more realistic, dynamic analysis of public goods provision would be vastly more complex and has yet to be developed, recent preliminary work in this direction suggests that there is greater scope for rational cooperation to provide public goods than the static model allows, but that it nevertheless remains true that voluntary cooperation to provide optimal amounts of public goods is less likely in relatively large groups than in smaller ones.[13]

The introduction of time in a more dynamic analysis of the process of public goods provision allows for the possibility of *conditional* cooperation. An individual can make his or her contribution to the provision of a public good conditional on others making contributions. He can, for example, refrain

[12] See, for example, John Chamberlin, 'Provision of collective goods as a function of group size', *American Political Science Review*, 68 (1974), 707–16; Taylor, *Anarchy and Cooperation*, ch. 2; and Russell Hardin, *Collective Action* (Baltimore: Johns Hopkins University Press for Resources for the Future, 1982), ch. 3.

[13] This was a conclusion of a grossly simplified dynamic analysis carried out in *Anarchy and Cooperation*, ch. 3.

from theft or from discharging wastes into a lake or from hunting whales, or he can make contributions to an organisation which seeks to get a public good provided, just as long as a sufficient number of others do. Such conditional cooperation can under certain conditions be rational, and if enough people cooperate conditionally, then the public good – some amount of it at any rate – gets provided.[14] Much voluntary cooperation in the provision of public goods is no doubt of this conditional kind. Unfortunately, it too is less likely to occur in large groups than in small ones, since a conditional cooperator must be able to monitor the behaviour of others in the group so as to reassure himself that they are doing their parts and not taking advantage of him. Clearly, as the size of the group increases, this mutual monitoring becomes increasingly difficult and the 'tacit contract' of conditional cooperation becomes increasingly fragile. In a relatively small group, on the other hand, especially one with an unchanging or only very slowly changing membership, people come into contact with and can observe the behaviour of most of their fellows, so that conditional cooperation is more likely to be workable. But even here, unless the group is *very* small, the arrangement is obviously a precarious one if it has no other supports. The nature of those supports will be discussed in Section 2.4.

2.2 Social order and the state

This argument – that people will not voluntarily cooperate to provide themselves with certain public goods if they are members of a large public – provides the foundation for an appealing justification of the state. The state, according to this liberal theory, is necessary because it alone can maintain

---

[14] For the details of one such analysis (which are too messy to be usefully summarised here) see *Anarchy and Cooperation*, ch. 3.

conditions in which contribution to the provision of public goods *is* rational, essentially by altering the structure of incentives facing potential free riders. The first full, explicit statement of this argument was set forth by Hobbes. He was the first to give a clear account of the free rider problem and to understand its importance for social and political life. The heart of his justification of the state has been accepted by many political theorists, though they all professed to reject his theory; and modern economists who have written about public goods generally take for granted the Hobbesian inference about the necessity or desirability of the state. The public goods Hobbes was concerned with were above all domestic order (in the sense of security of persons and their property) and also defence against foreign aggression. More recently, essentially the same argument has been made by a number of writers concerned with environmental problems. According to them, such public goods as cleaner air, rivers and lakes, control of population growth, protection of wilderness and maintenance of ecological diversity must be provided by the state or the state must ensure that people will cooperate to provide them. The persuasiveness of this justification of the state – and it has always been a popular one – lies in the fact that the state, on this view, exists to further *common* interests, to do what everybody wants done. Other arguments for the state, for example that income redistribution is desirable and can be achieved only through the intervention of the state, do not appeal to common interests – not, at any rate, in an obvious or uncontroversial way.[15]

As a justification of the state the liberal theory rests on shaky foundations and is fundamentally flawed. I have made this critical case in detail elsewhere (in *Anarchy and Cooperation*), but I

---

[15] The claim that redistribution is a public good is discussed in Section 3.2 below.

should like to summarise very briefly three of the arguments made in the earlier work because they are relevant to the argument of the rest of the present book. The first point is to do with the assumptions on which the entire liberal theory is founded. It is an essential feature of the theory that it takes individual preferences as given and fixed. In particular, it is effectively assumed that every individual is an egoist, in the sense that he is concerned solely with his own costs and benefits. He chooses not to contribute to the provision of a public good because the cost *to him* of making a contribution exceeds the benefit *to him* of the additional amount of the public good which could be provided out of his contribution. (In Hume's version of this justification of the state, individuals are assumed to be both egoistic and altruistic, but the altruism – in the form of 'private' and extensive benevolence – is effectively assumed to be sufficiently outweighed by the egoism for the resulting individual preference structures, when these also incorporate a discounting of future benefits, to make non-contribution to the provision of public goods the rational course of action. Interestingly, Hume anticipates the 'size' argument of Olson's *Logic of Collective Action* and makes it clear in the *Treatise* that his argument applies only to *large* societies, several times proclaiming his belief that the members of small societies may live without government – though the belief seems to be based in large part on his view that small societies tend to be 'uncultivated', that is, lacking very many possessions to quarrel about.)[16] Clearly, if an individual is sufficiently altruistic (in the sense of attaching some weight to others' benefits as well as his own), the total benefit (to himself and others) of contributing will exceed his costs, and therefore he will contribute. In other words, Olson's argument and the

---

[16] I have discussed this, and Hume's justification of government generally, in *Anarchy and Cooperation*, ch. 6.

liberal theory of the state critically depend on the assumption
that individuals are pure egoists or at least are 'insufficiently'
altruistic; with enough altruism, this rationale for the state
evaporates. It might be thought that this observation is
irrelevant or of theoretical interest only, for we have only to
look around us (at the amount of violence and robbery, or at
environmental pollution and resource depletion, for example)
to see that people are *not* sufficiently altruistic because they do
not in fact cooperate in the provision of public goods. It may be
the case, however, that this lack of altruism (at least in public
goods interaction) is in part the product of state intervention –
that it characterises people who have for a long time lived
under states. In *Anarchy and Cooperation* I argued that this is in
fact the case; and that preferences change over time as a result
of the activities of the state. Now if the state is in part the cause
of changes in individual preferences, then clearly it cannot be
deduced from the structure of preferences in the absence of the
state that the state is desirable (as is done in the liberal theory);
for the state modifies, one might say, the assumptions from
which its desirability has been deduced. If individual preferences
change over time, the question of the desirability (or 'prefera-
bility') of the state becomes much more complex than it is in
the static liberal theory; and if preferences change as a result of
the state itself, then it is not even clear what is *meant* by the
desirability of the state.[17] Any theory which attempts to justify
or recommend or prescribe an institution, practice, rule, new
technology or whatever, by reference to fixed, given preferences
(for example, by arguing that the institution, or whatever, is, in
terms of the given preferences, unanimously preferred to the

[17] An analogous point has been made about methods of social choice by
Kenneth Arrow, who nevertheless bases his work on the assumption that
individual preferences are not affected by the decision process itself. See his
Social Choice and Individual Values, 2nd edition (New York: Wiley, 1963),
pp. 7–8.

status quo or one which ensures Pareto-optimal outcomes) falls foul of the same fundamental objection, if the object to be justified has some effect over time on the individual preferences. Much of neo-classical welfare economics is vitiated by this objection.[18] I am not objecting here to the use of the assumption of pure egoism in *explanatory* theories, at least not those which are narrowly circumscribed (especially temporally) in the scope of their application. Without this assumption, or one close to it, it would indeed be hard to understand why, amongst other things, so many public goods are under-supplied. I am objecting to its use in 'normative' theories – theories which seek to justify or prescribe.

It seems to me that this general argument clearly applies to the liberal (or perhaps we should say 'neo-classical') theory of the state, for it would be hard to deny that individual preferences are affected, at least in the long run, by the state.

The second argument against the liberal justification of the state also concerns a dynamic effect and it is that the state tends to undermine the conditions which make the alternative to it workable, and in this way makes itself more desirable. It does this by weakening or destroying *community*, which is, as I shall argue, a necessary condition for the maintenance of social order without the state. Of course states were not alone in contributing to the decline of community. In particular, in the modern period it is difficult to disentangle the contributions of the growth of the state and the expansion of capitalism. But certainly the state, almost by definition, undermined communities by displacing many of the local activities once accomplished through reciprocity (one of the three core characteristics of community: see Section 1.4) by various forms of central

---

[18] Herbert Gintis argues something like this in 'A radical analysis of welfare economics and individual development', *Quarterly Journal of Economics*, 86 (1972), 572–99, and in 'Welfare criteria with endogenous preferences: the economics of education', *International Economic Review*, 15 (1974), 415–30.

mediation, including centralised redistributive, welfare and insurance activities and the provision of a range of public goods (local as well as national).[19] As part of this process, the formation – in the face of centuries of 'tenacious and widespread resistance' – of the modern national states in Europe involved 'co-opting, subordinating or destroying' village councils and other deliberative assemblies and 'abridging, destroying or absorbing' a variety of rights previously lodged in less inclusive political units, including the right of households to pasture animals on the village common and the right of the head of the household to punish its members.[20] We shall see in Section 3.3 that at the very origin of the state the normal process of fission, which characterises all stateless societies and ensures that they remain small communities, is halted because it has become impossible or unattractive for part of the community to split off and establish a replicate community elsewhere. This containment of the normal centrifugal forces, which results in a community growing in size or being absorbed into another community and losing its autonomy, is a central part of the process of state formation and growth; and although the constituent communities are eventually assimilated to each other culturally (through increasing communication, trade and so on, and through the efforts usually taken by the state to institute a common language, religion, legal system, educational curriculum, etc.), the resulting society becomes too large to be a community in anything except a very weak sense: direct and many-sided relations and the practice of reciprocity are not possible on a large scale.

The third criticism of the liberal justification of the state

---

[19] Reciprocity, it should be remembered, is not the same thing as altruism (though it involves short-term altruism) or charity or benevolence.

[20] Charles Tilly, 'Reflections on the history of European state-making', in Tilly, ed., *The Formation of National States in Western Europe* (Princeton, NJ: Princeton University Press, 1975), especially at pp. 21–4, 37 and 71.

which is relevant to the argument of this book concerns the concluding step in the justification. Even if the premises of the theory are accepted and even if we accept too the argument that the members of large publics will not voluntarily provide themselves with public goods – including the fundamental public good of social order – it does not follow that the state is the *only* means of ensuring the supply of such goods or that other means would not suffice and must be supplemented by the state. All that can be inferred is that, if public goods are to be provided, *some* means must be found of getting people to do their part in providing them.

Broadly speaking, three 'methods' have been proposed for ensuring the provision of the public good of social order. In practice the methods are found in various combinations. To characterise them briefly, they are: the state, the market and the community. The claim that social order can be satisfactorily provided by private firms competing in the marketplace is the subject of the next section. I then turn to the third, communitarian anarchist, method which is my main concern.

2.3 *Social order on the market*

The last two sections of this chapter will give an account of how social order is maintained in stateless societies and argue that social order without the state can be maintained only in community. I shall not take very seriously the claim that the *market* is an alternative to the state as a sole means of ensuring the provision of social order. The less radical claim, made by many laissez-faire liberals, that *some* of the goods whose provision constitutes social order can be put on the market, has, I think, some validity. But the full claim, made especially in the United States by people calling themselves 'anarcho-capitalists' or 'libertarians', that *all* the components of social order could be satisfactorily put on the market is in my view indefensible. In market societies, social order is maintained by a combination of 'state', 'community' and 'market'; and whereas order was once well-maintained in societies lacking states and markets, and in certain contemporary societies is imperfectly maintained principally (though never quite wholly) by the state, I doubt that it could be very successfully maintained in any societies by markets alone.

The argument which I shall make about social order and community shares with the liberal argument about social order and the state a common starting point, namely that there are significant externalities associated with the provision of social order and hence there is potentially a free rider problem. Libertarians generally minimise the importance of these externalities or even deny their existence altogether. They do not deny the existence of *all* externalities or that *some* goods are public. It is, for example, admitted by some libertarians that there would be a problem in an anarcho-capitalist society about national defence because it provides, amongst other things, a public good. The solutions they give to this particular public goods problem are unconvincing, though they have offered more plausible solutions to the problems of providing certain other public goods. It is suggested, for example, that an entrepreneur would get each member of the relevant public to sign a contract committing him to contributing to the provision of the public good on condition that every other member participates.[21] The trouble with this and other proposals is that they are likely to work only in very small publics (smaller even than the communities discussed below).[22]

But so far as social order and many other public goods are

---

[21] David Friedman, *The Machinery of Freedom*, ch. 34.

[22] In part for the same reasons (mentioned earlier) that conditional cooperation in the provision of public goods is less likely as the size of the public increases. Friedman admits (in *The Machinery of Freedom*) that all his proposals suffer from this size difficulty.

concerned, the libertarian view is that, if private property rights are greatly extended, rigorously defined and strictly defended, there would be no externalities or there would be a great reduction in activities with external costs.[23] Thus, if streets were in private hands, their owners would (it is assumed) have an interest in keeping them safe. If they were owned jointly by the landlords of rented property on them, it would pay the landlords to have order maintained on them because this would increase demand for their property and increase their incomes from rents. Similarly, traders who owned the street they operated on would pay to keep order on it. Or, if streets but not the properties on them were owned by 'street companies', the companies would charge the property owners for maintaining the streets and their safety, and the profits and stock values of these companies would depend on their providing a good service.[24]

In these libertarian proposals the protection of person and property is to be provided of course by private firms – 'protection agencies' – and a central claim of most libertarian accounts is that in the absence of the state a market in protection services would arise which would be and would remain *competitive*. The market would therefore be efficient. The competing firms would provide people with just the amounts and types of security they wanted. The inefficiency, corruption and brutality found in the state police forces would be bad for business (whereas state police forces continue to get

---

[23] If, for example, lakes, rivers and seas were privately owned, then according to this argument potential polluters would be deterred by the high costs they would have to pay (by prior agreement or in court). If every individual's property rights in his or her own body were rigorously defined and defended, there would be far less air pollution. And so on. 'Only private property rights will ensure an end to pollution-invasion of resources' – Murray Rothbard, *For a New Liberty; the Libertarian Manifesto*, revised edition (New York: Collier, 1978), p. 203.

[24] Cf. Rothbard, *For a New Liberty*, ch. 11, and Friedman, *The Machinery of Freedom*, ch. 15.

paid no matter what sort of service they provide). And when two protection agencies come into conflict in defence of their respective clients' grievances, it would not pay them to shoot it out; they would take their problem to arbitration (there would be a market in firms specialising in arbitration, and even, in some libertarian schemes, a market in systems of law). And so on.

This is the competitive scenario favoured by libertarians who are also anarcho-capitalists. Other libertarians are less sanguine about the likely outcome of competition between protection agencies, and admit that the prospect of violence between them (and other problems peculiar to the provision of order and defence) make necessary a minimal state whose sole function is the provision of internal and external security; or they argue, as Robert Nozick has done in *Anarchy, State and Utopia*, that the upshot of competition between protection agencies would be the emergence in each area of a single dominant protection agency (a proto-state, in effect, but not a state), since every individual, if he wanted to buy protection at all, would gravitate towards the largest firm, for this would tend to come out on top in disputes with smaller firms. According to another monopolistic scenario, which in Brian Barry's view is more plausible than Nozick's and in fact 'corresponds closely to a commonly found reality', an agency declares that it will 'represent the collective interests of Aryans against Jews, settlers against aboriginal inhabitants, whites against blacks, Protestants against Catholics, or any other against others', always supporting a member of the privileged group in a dispute against a member of an excluded group and perhaps even preventing excluded groups from forming their own protection agencies.[25]

[25] Brian Barry, review of Robert Nozick, *Anarchy, State and Utopia*, *Political Theory*, 3 (1975), 331–6.

Is the market in protection of persons and their property, in the absence of a state, likely to be competitive or monopolistic or oligopolistic? If one of the last two, what sort of restrictive business practices, if any, are firms likely to engage in? Will the protection agencies be as well-behaved as the anarcho-capitalists suppose? I don't think that any of these questions can be answered with confidence. The right sort of evidence just isn't there. Oligopoly is in fact the commonest market form in the industrial West and near-monopoly is common, but the libertarians would argue (with some justice in many cases) that these market structures survive only with the help of the state. There are, furthermore, already extensive markets in security services in some countries,[26] with firms contracting to protect individuals, factories, art galleries, office-blocks, department stores and other premises, to collect debts and pursue adulterous spouses, to transport cash, bullion and other valuables, and so on. But the nature of these markets and the behaviour of the firms operating in them cannot provide reliable evidence of the kind required to judge the libertarians' claim, since the markets are not free: they are subject to government regulation and operate only in areas neglected by the state's police forces or as a supplement to them. In England, at any rate, this (regulated and truncated) market in security seems to be fairly competitive, but the personnel and methods of many firms are apparently such as to cast doubt on the optimistic scenarios of the anarcho-capitalists. A recent survey of private police in the United Kingdom[27] quotes from an article in the *Police Review* of March 1972 by Chief Inspector Sydney Pleece, who writes that, in the estimation of the Metropolitan Crime Prevention Branch, 'of about 150–200 medium to very small companies offering

---

[26] There are currently about as many private policemen in England as there are in the regular police force. See Hilary Draper, *Private Police* (Harmondsworth: Penguin, 1978), p. 23.

[27] Draper, *Private Police*, p. 117.

various security services in the Metropolis, some 30–40 *per cent* are to be regarded as dubious, either because the principals have criminal records or employ men with such records or because of limited ability, equipment or unsatisfactory selling methods'.

Whether the market in security is competitive or not, its ability to supply the security people want will be seriously hampered by the presence of externalities. As I have said, libertarians generally minimise the importance of externalities in this area or deny their existence altogether. It is true that much of what goes to make up social order can be decomposed into particular *private* goods and that this fact is ignored by those who treat social order as a public good *tout court*. When I hire a firm to protect my person or house or factory, the firm's service benefits mainly myself. But even if the firm's agents decline to intervene when they see property being stolen from the house of my neighbour (who is not one of their clients), there is nevertheless *some* external benefit to others arising from my purchase of protection. For a protection agency, like the state, would have to provide security mainly by *deterring* theft and violence with threats that it would track down the offender and exact retribution (and of course it would have to try, at least some of the time, to carry out these threats when deterrence failed, so that the threats remained credible). Thus everyone in the area covered by the protection agency benefits from any individual's purchase of protection – *unless* the agencies all publish (or aspiring violators can otherwise obtain) a list of those persons who have bought no protection. Deterrence, then, is a non-excludable public good.[28] With or without this proviso about knowledge of the non-contributors, it is hard to see how, for example, a group of traders, who

---

[28] If a public good can be provided in an *excludable* mode and exclusion is not too costly, then competitive private production can be efficient. See Harold Demsetz, 'The private production of public goods', *Journal of Law and Economics*, 13 (1970), 293–306.

engage a firm to keep their street safe for customers, do not provide *some* benefit to others, including fellow-traders on their street who decline to contribute. In other words, there is, as I have already argued in other ways in Section 2.1, a non-excludable public good element in the provision of security; and therefore in general the market will not produce a Pareto-optimal outcome: individuals will not get all the security they want.

If the market in security is *not* competitive – if it consists mainly of a monopoly firm or of colluding oligopolists – then it will in any case resemble a state, being a repository of concentrated force and political specialisation. Finally, whether the market is competitive or not, it must be remembered that the product is a peculiar one: when we buy cars or shoes or telephone services we do not give the firm power based on force, but armed protection agencies, like the state, make customers (their own and others') vulnerable, and having given them power we cannot be sure that they will use it only for our protection.

2.4 Social order in stateless societies

I asserted earlier that, broadly speaking, there are three ways of ensuring the provision of the public good of social order, which can be summarily characterised as the state, the market and the community. Having rejected the market, I shall argue that the other alternative to the state, community, is in fact a necessary condition for the maintenance of stateless social order. I begin the argument in this section by looking at the range of means by which social order was in fact maintained in the stateless primitive societies and other quasi-anarchic societies introduced in Section 1.5. Most of these means of maintaining order are still to be found in modern societies with well-developed states, but in atrophied and attenuated forms.

The means of maintaining social order in primitive societies fall (though not very neatly) into three categories. In the first place there are of course the social controls proper, by which I mean the use of threats and offers (and throffers) of negative and positive sanctions. In the second category are the various processes of socialisation, which can be thought of as setting the stage for the use of the social controls by moulding the preferences which the threats and offers go to work on, as well as helping reduce a community's need to rely on them. And finally, certain basic structural characteristics of these societies contribute to or play a role in the maintenance of social order; they are not *specifically* mechanisms of social control and cannot be separated from what is controlled, but provide a framework in which the social controls can be used and establish conditions for their effectiveness. Let us consider these first.

The spirit of Marcel Mauss's celebrated essay on *The Gift* is that in primitive society peace and order is secured by reciprocal giving. For Marshall Sahlins, in his essays on Mauss and primitive exchange, this reciprocity apparently alone suffices to maintain social order. He writes, 'the gift is the primitive way of achieving peace that in civil society is secured by the State',[29] and he argues that Mauss's thinking bore a close resemblance to a central part of Hobbes's argument in *Leviathan*. Without the state, in the Hobbesian 'state of nature', there is a rough equality of vulnerability amongst individuals and they live without security of person and property, not necessarily fighting amongst themselves but with this potentiality ever present. So too, in primitive society, without gift-giving, Mauss saw a rough equality of force, though among groups rather than individuals, and an ever present predisposition to open fighting between them. Mauss wrote that 'To refuse to give, or to fail to invite is – like refusing to accept – the equivalent of a declaration of war; it is a refusal of friendship and intercourse',

[29] Marshall Sahlins, *Stone Age Economics*, p. 169.

and such refusals are made on pain of 'private or open warfare'. To get out and to stay out of this primitive 'state of nature', men 'learnt to renounce what was theirs and made contracts to give and repay', and, 'opposing reason to emotion', they succeeded in 'substituting alliance, gift and commerce for war, isolation and stagnation'.[30]

The reciprocity which Mauss and Sahlins believe to play a vital role in maintaining order refers presumably to a range of types of reciprocity corresponding to the generalised–balanced segment of Sahlins' spectrum – most often towards the generalised end.[31]

There is a strong correlation between the form of reciprocity and kinship distance: as the kinship distance separating two individuals increases, the more do relations between them incline towards the unsociable negative end of the spectrum. Kinship groups – and simultaneously residential groups, since kinsmen generally live near by and neighbours are kin – can be thought of as a series of nested sectors. Generalised reciprocity is confined to the household and local lineage sectors, balanced reciprocity mainly to the village and tribal sectors, and negative reciprocity to the intertribal sector. (The strength of this correlation between reciprocity and kinship will of course vary, and in particular the negative reciprocity usually characteristic of intertribal relations may be replaced by a more balanced reciprocity in cases where there is trading or other intertribal symbiosis.) Certainly, generalised reciprocity predominates in the acephalous hunting–gathering bands and in the household and local lineage sectors of those tribal societies which are stateless.[32]

---

[30] Marcel Mauss, *The Gift: Forms and Functions of Exchange in Archaic Societies* (London: Routledge and Kegan Paul, 1969), pp. 11, 13, 79–80. (French first edition, 1925.)

[31] See Section 1.4 above.

[32] See the appendices to ch. 5 of *Stone Age Economics* for examples, and for an especially interesting discussion of a hunting–gathering case see Lorna Marshall, 'Sharing, talking and giving: relief of social tensions among !Kung Bushmen', *Africa*, 31 (1961), 231–49.

How close in fact is the Maussian argument to Hobbes? What Sahlins has in mind in pointing to the resemblance between the two is Hobbes's argument that conditional cooperation (to produce the public good of social order) is rational in the state of nature. Hobbes's first or fundamental Law of Nature is *'That every man, ought to endeavour Peace, as farre forth as he has hope of obtaining it; and when he cannot obtain it, that he may seek, and use, all helps, and advantages of Warre'*, and from it is derived the second, *'That a man be willing, when others are so too, as farre-forth, as for Peace, and defence of himselfe, he shall think it necessary, to lay down his right to all things.'* Sahlins is right to see in this second law, and in the third (covenant-keeping) and fifth (mutual accommodation), an analogy with Mauss's reciprocity, though the congruence is far from precise, as we shall see. But the fourth law of nature, as he says, *is* very close to 'the gift'. This is the law of gratitude:

That a man which receiveth Benefit from another of meer Grace, Endeavour that he which giveth it, have no reasonable cause to repent him of his good will. For no man giveth, but with the intention of Good to himselfe; because Gift is Voluntary; and of all Voluntary Acts, the Object is to every man his own Good; of which if men see they shall be frustrated, there will be no beginning of benevolence, or trust; nor consequently of mutual help; nor of reconciliation of one man to another; and therefore they are to remain still in the condition of War . . .

Nevertheless, despite the obvious resemblance between the spirit of *The Gift* and a central (and often misunderstood) part of Hobbes's argument in *Leviathan*, there are important differences. In the first place, of course, Mauss and Sahlins certainly part company with Hobbes here if, as seems to be the case, they believe that 'the gift' is a *substitute* for the state, that by itself it can secure Peace. Conditional cooperation is rational for everyone, says Hobbes, but only if it is made safe by the state; so it is not a substitute for the state. But then Mauss and Sahlins are talking mainly about primitive society (although even in primitive society, reciprocity does not stand alone as a surrogate for the state). More importantly, generalised reciprocity (of which food sharing is perhaps the most widespread and frequently occurring instance) is not the same thing as the conditional cooperation central to Hobbes's argument – the mutual laying aside of the 'right of nature' ('the Liberty each man hath, to use his own power, as he will himselfe, for the preservation of his own Nature; that is to say, of his own Life; and consequently, of doing anything, which in his own Judgement, and Reason, hee shall conceive to be the aptest means thereunto'), which in practice means refraining from violence, theft, etc., or in more recent versions of the Hobbesian argument, refraining from such things as having 'too many' children, discharging untreated wastes into rivers and lakes, hunting whales and other species threatened with extinction, and so on. This is not to say that the reciprocity of which Mauss and Sahlins speak does not help to secure order (which it does in part by initiating and maintaining certain kinds of social relations); only that this is not exactly what Hobbes had in mind (except in the fourth law, 'gratitude', which, like the fourteen laws following it, stands in an unsatis-factorily loose relation to the crucial first three laws).

Within the household, the local lineage and the village, the most important kind of reciprocity is probably food sharing. Between local communities, lineages, clans and moieties, it is the *exchange of women in marriage*. In its simplest form (as practised, for example, by the Shoshone and Eskimo, who lived in families which temporarily united in bands for cooperative hunts or for winter settlement), the men of two families exchange sisters, so that a man's sister marries his wife's brother. The same form of exchange, continued over generations, serves also to unite patrilocal bands, as well as tribal lineages, clans and moieties. In some cases, bands are grouped into two moieties, a band of one moiety exchanging women with one or perhaps several bands of the opposite moiety. This type of exchange corresponds to bilateral cross-cousin marriage: a man marries his father's sister's daughter who is at the same time his mother's brother's daughter – though it is the exchange between groups which is important, marriage partners usually being only classificatory cross-cousins. In another form of exchange, corresponding to patrilateral cross-cousin marriage, a woman marries into the group from which her *mother* came; thus there is delayed exchange, in the sense that reciprocation is made in the following generation. All these exchange systems are direct or symmetrical: a woman is received from the group to which one was given. There are also indirect or asymmetrical systems, such as that corresponding to matrilateral cross-cousin marriage, in which a man receives a wife from one group or set of groups but gives wives to a different group or set of groups. Thus, in these systems, there are chains of wife-giving, which must be cyclical (for example: $A \rightarrow B \rightarrow C \rightarrow A$, or $A \rightarrow B \rightarrow C \rightarrow D \rightarrow A$ *and* $C \rightarrow A$), otherwise there would be wifeless wife-givers at one end of the chain and the system could not be perpetuated. Women are thus circulated rather than exchanged, but the whole set of groups involved is bound together nevertheless.[33]

The exchange of women in marriage creates and cements bonds between individuals and groups. 'Among tribes of low culture', wrote Edward B. Tylor, 'there is but one means known of keeping up permanent alliance, and that means is inter-marriage ... Again and again in the world's history, savage tribes must have had plainly before their minds the simple practical alternative between marrying-out and being killed

[33] For an excellent introduction to marital alliance theory, see Robin Fox, *Kinship and Marriage* (Harmondsworth: Penguin, 1967), chs. 7 and 8.

out.'[34] But it is not just as a form of reciprocity that exchange of women contributes to peace and order; it does so as well because it helps to create the conflicting loyalties which result from the *crosscutting* of marital and other ties. In a dispute between two individuals from groups which exchange women in marriage, each man's primary loyalty may be to his own group but the zeal with which he and co-members of his group pursue his claim will be diminished because of their affinal ties with the other group. Of course, clan exogamy or local group exogamy or any other form of exogamy practised by groups will create crosscutting ties, but in the absence of a positive marriage rule (an 'elementary' marriage system) these ties presumably are weaker, as they bear on disputes between any two particular groups, though they link a group to a greater number of other groups. In elementary marriage systems (of the kinds mentioned above, for example), groups are perpetually allied and are bound together by more links than in the case of 'complex' marriage systems having rules of exogamy but otherwise no positive rules specifying marriage partners.

Two other important sources of conflicting loyalties are clans and age-groups. Clans, especially in segmentary tribes, are very often geographically dispersed, with members of several clans in each local community, which is an amalgam of lineage branches of different clans. Division into clans is thus a cleavage which crosscuts division into local communities, and in a dispute between members of different communities a man's loyalties may be divided between loyalty to his local community and loyalty to his clan brothers.

In very many tribes, age-sets and age-grades, into which males are recruited on the basis of age or generation, serve to unite males irrespective of descent or residence or both. Thus,

---

[34] Edward B. Tylor, 'On a method of investigating the development of institutions: applied to laws of marriage and descent', *Journal of the Royal Anthropological Institute*, 18 (1888), 245–67.

loyalties to age-mates conflict in these cases with loyalties to kin or the local community. If, unusually, members of an age-set form a separate local community (as with the so-called age-villages of the Nyakyusa),[35] then kin are dispersed, so that there is crosscutting between kinship on the one hand and the mutually reinforcing age and residence cleavages on the other. The rites of initiation from boyhood into manhood, which in many cases mark the creation of the age-sets, may have special significance as part of another means of social control which will be discussed below.

In a society characterised by patrilineal descent but matrilocal post-marital residence, descent and residence give rise to crosscutting cleavages. The same of course is true of matrilineal, patrilocal societies and indeed there will be some degree of crosscutting in any society where residential groups do not correspond to or are not closely based upon descent groups – as they cannot be where there are, for example, cognatic (or bilateral) descent groups, unless these are of the restricted type, or where there are double (or dual) descent groups.[36] But there is a crucial difference, where the maintenance of order is concerned, between matrilocal and patrilocal systems. It is always a group of closely related men which is responsible for coming to the defence of an aggrieved person and which in particular must exact vengeance if one of its members is killed. This group has been referred to as a 'fraternal interest group' and as the 'vengeance group'. In a patrilocal system it is

[35] Monica Wilson, *Good Company: A Study of Nyakyusa Age-Villages* (London: Oxford University Press, 1951).

[36] Fox, *Kinship and Marriage*, chs. 5 and 6. Note that crosscutting between residence groups and descent groups is not the same thing as that referred to earlier in connection with marital exchange systems. In a patrilineal, patrilocal society where local communities are based on descent groups, there is no crosscutting of residence and descent groups, but there are of course affinal links between the local communities. The effect on peace and order of this latter type of crosscutting (if it deserves the name), and the conflict of loyalties it engenders, is presumably weaker than the effect of the crosscutting of residential and descent groups.

localised, hence able to spring into action and more likely to act than in a matrilocal system where its members are dispersed. Thus, matrilocality contributes to the maintenance of peace and order. So too, though presumably not to the same degree, do neo-local, ambilocal and other residence rules which disperse the vengeance group.[37]

Once mutual hostilities are under way, crosscutting cleavages often serve to temper or terminate them. Indeed it is doubtful that a society could long survive under a system of self-help retaliation and vengeance if it were not for extensive cross-cutting of important cleavages. Crosscutting becomes particularly important whenever, as is often the case, the individual parties to a dispute are supported by *groups* (usually comprising their close kinsmen). In this case, the dispute is enlarged and is therefore potentially more disruptive, but this has the effect of making it more likely that a disputant will have ties of loyalty to the other side as well as to his own group, and hence there will be more individuals with a desire to end the dispute.

A special case of this massing of groups behind individuals in conflict is the 'complementary opposition' characteristic of 'segmentary lineage societies'. 'The segmentary lineage system consists of this: the focal lines of primary segments can be placed on a single agnatic genealogy that accounts for much (all, in the Tiv case) of the tribe. The closer the genealogical relation between focal lines, the closer their respective segments

---

[37] A clear correlation between matrilocality and peacefulness was found in a cross-cultural test by H. U. E. Thoden van Velzen and W. van Wetering: 'Residence, power groups and intra-societal aggression', *International Archives of Ethnology*, 49 (1960), 169–200. See also K. F. and C. S. Otterbein, 'An eye for an eye, a tooth for a tooth: a cross-cultural study of feuding', *American Anthropologist*, 67 (1965), 1470–82, and G. E. Kang, 'Conflicting loyalties theory: a cross-cultural test', *Ethnology*, 15 (1976), 201–10. Unfortunately, these last two studies of crosscutting substitute 'feuding' (defined as blood-revenge following a homicide) for violence. On crosscutting and social order, see generally Max Gluckman, *Custom and Conflict in Africa* (Oxford: Blackwell, 1955), ch. 1, and Elizabeth Colson, 'Social control and vengeance in Plateau Tonga society', *Africa*, 23 (1953), 199–212.

are on the ground.'[38] The idea of complementary opposition is, very roughly speaking, that of a society divided into sections, each subdivided into subsections, and each of these divided into primary segments (the Nuer villages or Tiv minimal *tar*, for example), such that in a dispute between two men from different 'villages' each man is supported by all the men of his respective village (and nobody else is involved), but if a man from one of these villages is in dispute with a man from any village of a different tribal subsection, then each man's subsection will drop any internal quarrels and unite behind him in opposition to the other subsection. Similarly for disputes involving men of different sections. This principle of complementary opposition operates in different forms in all societies,[39] but is not important in many of them as far as the maintenance of order is concerned; and though a wide variety of societies were once thought to be of the segmentary lineage type (and some writers seemed almost to equate 'segmentary lineage society' with 'stateless society'), it is now realised that the only fairly pure examples are the Tiv and the Nuer.

It is an exaggeration to claim, as Southall does, that 'the order, balance and equilibrium that obtain throughout a society as perceived by its members depend largely on the complementary opposition of groups and categories of varying permanence'.[40] It seems to me that what the complementary opposition mechanism (with its correlative 'segmentary soli-

---

[38] Marshall Sahlins, 'The segmentary lineage: an organization of predatory expansion', *American Anthropologist*, 63 (1961), 332–45. This article gives an excellent brief exposition of the segmentary lineage system. See also Laura Bohannan, 'Political aspects of Tiv social organization', in J. Middleton and D. Tait, eds., *Tribes Without Rulers* (London: Routledge and Kegan Paul, 1958).

[39] As M. G. Smith has emphasised: 'On segmentary lineage systems', *Journal of the Royal Anthropological Institute*, 86 (1956), 39–80.

[40] Adrian Southall, 'Stateless society', *International Encyclopedia of the Social Sciences* (1968), vol. 15, pp. 157–68. Even if crosscutting is to be included with complementary opposition proper (as Southall seems to assume) this is still, I think, an exaggeration.

darity') does perhaps contribute to order is to ensure that whenever there is a dispute between individuals it will always be escalated to a dispute between groups and, furthermore, these groups will always be of approximately equal strength. The results of this balanced massing of opposing groups are, first, to make a dispute more serious, the consequences of actual fighting much nastier, and hence to introduce a more powerful deterrent to causing disputes; second, by calling forth two approximately equal groups, to ensure that the deterrence is mutual; and third, to increase the amount of interrelatedness between the two sides, hence to introduce or intensify a conflict of loyalties, which increases the pressures brought to bear to terminate the dispute. Complementary opposition calls to mind certain features of contemporary international relations. When it fails to act as a deterrent, it serves to escalate the conflict, which presumably does not in itself promote peace and order.

The means of maintaining social order so far discussed are in effect aspects of the social structure. They are not *specifically* mechanisms of social control and cannot be separated from what is controlled. In this fundamental respect they differ from such characteristic instruments of social control in societies with a well-developed state as police and prisons. Malinowski brought this out well in his studies of the Trobriand Islanders when he wrote that 'law' and 'legal phenomena' (by which he meant, in effect, the means by which social order is maintained) 'do not consist in any independent institutions'. They represent 'rather an aspect of their tribal life, one side of their structure, than any independent, self-contained social arrangements' and are 'the specific result of the configuration of obligations, which makes it impossible for the native to shirk his responsibility without suffering for it in the future'.[41] And in an

---

[41] Bronislaw Malinowski, *Crime and Custom in Savage Society* (London: Routledge and Kegan Paul, 1926), pp. 58–9.

acephalous primitive society his sufferings will often be considerable and prolonged – because his deviant behaviour *ramifies*, disrupting normal social life all around him. This in turn is the result of what Nadel has called the 'multivalence' of social activities and of what Southall calls the 'multiplexity' of social relations.[42] The multivalence of a social activity is its capacity 'to serve also ends or interests other than the one for which it is explicitly or primarily designed', so that deviation from it has the effect of frustrating this whole range of interests, and the prospect of this serves to inhibit deviation. The multiplexity of social relations results from the lack of specialised roles characteristic of these stateless societies. Activities are not compartmentalised; relations between people are multifaceted; the individual does not interact with distinct groups of people for different purposes. In such societies there are, in particular, no specialised political or economic roles, and there are no activities which are *only* economic or political. Activities which are 'primarily' economic (if indeed one can talk of the economic at all), for example exchange characterised by generalised reciprocity, serve other ends as well, as we have seen; they are multivalent. It follows that 'neither economic nor political ends can be exclusively pursued by anyone to the detriment of society'.[43]

On the role played by socialisation and education in the maintenance of social order, I can be brief. Evidently there is a simple sense in which education and socialisation are fundamental to social order, since the values they inculcate (some of them at least) are presupposed by other means of control and there must obviously be a large measure of agreement on some

---

[42] S. F. Nadel, 'Social control and self-regulation', *Social Forces*, 3 (1953), 265–73; Southall, 'Stateless society'.
[43] Southall, 'Stateless society'.

matters if controls are to be effective in the absence of concentrated force and a division of political labour. Ridicule and shaming devices, for example, could not have their effect (to be, discussed below) unless people had the appropriate values and emotions. But in my view it does not make much sense to single out socialisation for the central role in the maintenance of social order, to claim, as Morton Fried does, that 'in all societies the single most significant complex of social-control apparatuses is to be found in the system of education, including both formal and informal means'.[44] The use of the devices of ridiculing and shaming – and the practice of all the other methods of control considered here – itself contributes to the socialisation of individuals. But there are of course negative sanctions associated with these devices and the use of the tacit threats to implement them is manifestly necessary in the maintenance of order. The same goes for the positive and negative sanctions associated with other controls. In other words, although the way in which children are brought up obviously can make an important difference to their behaviour as adults,[45] socialisation is not enough.

It has been suggested that age-grading initiation ceremonies or 'puberty rites' are a phase of the process of socialisation which plays a particularly important part in the maintenance of social order, since by associating great physical pain with lectures on the standards expected of an adult member of the community, it is ensured that these standards will never be forgotten and hence will be conformed to. Ronald Berndt relates that among the people (Kamano, Fore, Usurufa and Jaté) he studied in the eastern Highlands of New Guinea, the

---

[44] Morton H. Fried, *The Evolution of Political Society* (New York: Random House, 1967), p. 9.
[45] For some interesting examples of this from primitive peoples (especially hunters and gatherers), see Ashley Montagu, ed., *Learning Non-Aggression* (New York: Oxford University Press, 1978).

following operations are performed serially on the novice
during the initiation ceremonies: his nasal septum is pierced
with a salt-smeared bamboo sliver which is then twirled around
in the hole; his tongue is cut; some of his fingers are pierced
under the nail; his nose is bled by forcing several salt-smeared
leaves of pipit cane up his nostrils and twirling them about;
later his penis is bled by having forced into it first 'spear' grass,
then a twig, then leaves bunched together; and finally the apex
of his penis is cut with a bamboo knife and a sharpened bone
from a pig's leg is inserted into the penis, then replaced by
bundles of leaves which are forced up and twirled around.[46]
During these rites the novices are subjected also to harangues
on what is expected of them as adults. The Aranda bands of
Australia subjected their initiates to subincision – the final
stage of several weeks of ordeals. A long thin bone was inserted
into the urethra and the penis split open by hacking down to
the bone with a piece of flint. The aboriginal Luiseño bands of
Southern California required their novices 'to lie motionless
while being bitten repeatedly by hordes of angry ants', amongst
other things, and 'as ordeal passed to new ordeal throughout
the ceremony, the candidate received long lectures on proper
conduct, on how to become a man of value, and on the religious
practices of his band'.[47]

There may be something in this argument about the importance of these rites and their accompanying lectures in the
maintenance of social order, but there are a number of
problems with it. First, there is the awkward fact that the
lectures delivered during the initiation ceremonies may in
some societies (those studied by Berndt, for example) place
great emphasis on competitive, aggressive, fighting and other

[46] Ronald M. Berndt, *Excess and Restraint: Social Control Among a New Guinea People*
(Chicago: University of Chicago Press, 1962).
[47] Peter Farb, *Man's Rise to Civilisation as Shown by the Indians of North America from
Primeval Times to the Coming of the Industrial State* (London: Paladin, 1971), p. 72.

qualities hardly conducive to the maintenance of order. Second, though it is indeed plausible that the lessons (whether cooperative and pacific, or otherwise) learned in association with such memorable ordeals will not be quickly forgotten, it does not follow that the norms enjoined by them will be adhered to. If, however, socialisation also results in a well-developed sense of guilt and sensitivity to ridicule and shaming, then well-remembered norms would indeed be effective in the maintenance of order (provided the norms are of an appropriate sort). Third, even if comparisons are limited to stateless societies, there is great variation – which needs to be explained – in the severity of the initiation ordeals, in the proportion of youths who have to submit to them, in the nature and amount of the accompanying indoctrination (in some societies there is none at all) and in the extent of initiation of girls. The Kuma of the New Guinea Highlands, for example, have much in common with the nearby communities studied by Berndt but their male initiation ceremonies are much less prolonged and harsh and do not affect all youths uniformly, for they are held at long intervals and there is great variation in the youths' ages at initiation and in the extent of participation in the various rites and lectures (some youths, chiefly because of their age, do not participate at all). The ethnographer offers no evidence to suggest (and appears not to believe) that it is those who escape the ordeals and the lectures who grow up to be the non-conformists, though she does claim that the result of this uneven socialisation at the time of initiation is more diversity and less conformity in adult behaviour.[48] In Nuer society, to take another example, the rites of initiation to manhood undergone by all males include 'a very severe operation' in which their brows are cut to the bone several times from ear to ear, but, says Evans-Pritchard, 'there is no purposive education or moral training in the procedure of initiation'.[49]

Even if in many societies the ceremonies and rituals associated with the passage to adulthood do not contribute much to the process of socialisation by joining great physical pain to explicit lectures on the social behaviour of an adult, they may nevertheless play a part in socialisation simply by emphasising – sometimes, as we have seen, rather dramatically – the initiate's accession to a new status, which of course makes him a full member of the community with well-defined obligations and responsibilities. And in general there is little doubt that the rituals and ceremonies of primitive societies – marking seasonal changes, life crises and the installation of chiefs and headmen – reinforce socialisation by symbolising the social structure and reaffirming the norms and beliefs of the society, and cooperation in their performance requires people to be at peace with one another.[50] This 'ritual superintegration' extends beyond the limits of the political unit, uniting bands, lineages, clans or other groups recognising no common authority.

I come now to the social controls proper. Before considering each of them in turn, a general point should be noted. Recall that in a pure anarchy there is no concentration of force and no

[48] Marie Reay, *The Kuma: Freedom and Conformity in the New Guinea Highlands* (Melbourne: University Press, 1959). Farb (*Man's Rise to Civilisation*, p. 73) cites with approval the argument that the severity of initiation rites varies with the harshness of the environment, the rites being most severe where a particularly harsh environment makes a precarious survival dependent upon minimising anti-social behaviour. The argument appears to be based on a comparison of the subincising Aranda with other Australian aborigines who live in better circumstances on the coast and who merely do such things as pound out one of the initiate's teeth; it looks less secure when, for example, some of the relatively well-placed New Guinea Highlands societies are brought in to the comparison. Besides, it is not clear that survival *is* precarious for the hunter-gatherers of harsh environments. For a discussion of the evidence, see Sahlins, 'The original affluent society', in *Stone Age Economics*.

[49] E. E. Evans-Pritchard, *The Nuer* (Oxford: Clarendon Press, 1940), pp. 249 and 253.

[50] See Max Gluckman, *Politics, Law and Ritual in Tribal Society* (Oxford: Blackwell, 1977), ch. 11; Victor W. Turner, *The Ritual Process* (Chicago: Aldine, 1969).

political speçialisation. Thus, in a *pure* anarchy nobody is denied participation in whatever means are used to maintain social order, and in particular no individual or group is denied the use of force, or of threats to use force, in seeking to redress a grievance, retaliate wrongs or deter others from committing them. In the primitive anarchies which are the closest historical or prehistorical approximations to this theoretical ideal of pure anarchy, there is some concentration of the use of force (in the hands of adult males) and there is a minimal division of political labour, though the specialists are not backed by organised force, so cannot enforce their decisions throughout the community. In the primitive anarchies, then, we should find wide participation in the processes of social control and in the use of force or of threats to use force, wherever these are used. This is indeed the case.

Unsurprisingly, then, a basic social control in primitive stateless societies is the threat of retaliation – 'self-help justice' carried out against the offender (and perhaps also his close kinsmen) by his victim or the victim assisted by his close kinsmen or, if the victim is dead or incapacitated, by his kinsmen alone. One form of this is the feud – a relation governed by recognised rules between groups of kinsmen, continuing through generations and in some cases interminable, and consisting eventually if not immediately in exchanges of homicide. The growth of the state (see Section 3.3 below) must by definition entail the removal of the right to pursue feuds and other forms of violent retaliation by offended individuals and groups, so that 'with rare exceptions . . . the practice of feud . . . is confined to societies in which there is little or no instituted "civil government"'.[51]

Clearly the practice of the feud itself does little to enhance

---

[51] Jacob Black-Michaud, *Cohesive Force: Feud in the Mediterranean and the Middle East* (Oxford: Blackwell, 1975), p. 146.

the security of persons and their property; but the *fear* of incurring violent retaliation and perhaps precipitating a feud is itself a potent deterrent from violence and theft. Among the Nuer, in Evans-Pritchard's view, 'fear of incurring a blood-feud is, in fact, the most important legal sanction within a tribe and the main guarantee of an individual's life and property'.[52] There is of course some similarity between this mechanism of social control and the state, inasmuch as control is afforded in both cases by the threat of retaliation by force; but there are fundamental differences, most notably that the 'self-help' system, as it is practised in stateless societies, is much more egalitarian.

I have already written on the role which reciprocal giving plays in maintaining social order by initiating and sustaining friendly social intercourse. I want now to emphasise briefly that the system of reciprocity is also an important source of social control. Food sharing and the pooling and exchange of labour, especially in certain hunting, fishing, horticultural and agricultural operations, are highly valued forms of aid which are given conditionally. Without them the individual would generally be materially much worse off and in some cases unable to subsist. So he is faced with a throffer, a threat and offer combined: if he does his part and if he refrains from anti-social behaviour, he will continue to receive reciprocal aid; otherwise it will be withdrawn. Malinowski in his studies of the Trobriand Islands was the first to give a central place to the role of this throffer in the maintenance of social order.[53] Some would say that he attached too great an importance to it, to the neglect of other means of maintaining order, but there is no doubt that this ever present throffer is one very potent form of social control.

[52] Evans-Pritchard, *The Nuer*, p. 150.
[53] Malinowski, *Crime and Custom in Savage Society*, especially Part I, chs. 3–5.

Less serious sanctions than the withdrawal of reciprocal aid but ones which nevertheless play a part in maintaining social order in stateless primitive societies are the various forms and degrees of ostracism and excommunication. By ostracism I mean only the exclusion of an individual from everyday social intercourse and withdrawal of courtesy and company, and by excommunication the exclusion from participation in rituals.[54] An individual can be subjected to either or both of these without at the same time being denied the benefits of reciprocity, or all three forms of sanction may be applied together.

Ostracism and excommunication and the withdrawal of reciprocity between them cover a range of sanctions which consist in the denial of benefits of different aspects of social interaction. An extreme sanction of this kind is expulsion from the community, a sanction which is rarely used in most primitive societies and not found at all in some. Its severity depends of course on the expelled individual's prospects of being received into another community and his likely standing in it. In some societies expulsion is a virtual death sentence; in others, there are a small number of other communities which might accept him, but he will suffer there from being stigmatised as one who has been expelled (or has had to flee) from his home community.

The positive and negative sanctions associated with the giving and withdrawal of reciprocal aid, with 'self-help' violent retaliation, and with ostracism, excommunication and expulsion, all of course *result* from and give expression to approval and disapproval; but they are to be distinguished from approval and disapproval, which are themselves sources of satisfaction and suffering and so can be sanctions in their own right. Offers and

[54] For examples of excommunication, see Christoph von Fürer-Haimendorf, *Morals and Merit: A Study of Values and Social Controls in South Asian Societies* (London: Weidenfeld and Nicolson, 1967), e.g. at pp. 49–50 and 123–6.

threats to give and withhold approval, esteem, respect, and so on, can have a deterrent effect independently of threats and offers using these other sanctions, and approval and disapproval need not give rise to them. Disapproval may give rise to shame and a sense of guilt – the rough distinction between these being that a person can feel *guilt* privately, without others knowing of its cause, whereas *shame* is felt as a result of disapprobation, so presupposes consciousness of public exposure. Some writers (but not including anthropologists) appear to believe that in primitive societies the sanctions of disapproval, guilt and shame are alone responsible for maintaining social order – or what little of it that is not already explained (by them) as an automatic outcome of dire poverty. It is true that these sanctions, which make a contribution to order in every society, are much more important in those small, face-to-face communities in which the individual is well-known to most others, typically expects to spend his entire life, and is usually dependent on the goodwill of others for vital economic cooperation; and it is reported of the members of most stateless societies that they are highly sensitive to the opinions of those around them and have an easily excited sense of shame. But, as the whole of this section makes plain, this set of sanctions is only one of the means by which order is maintained in primitive anarchies and there is no basis for arguing that it is in some sense the most important or most potent.

In addition to gossip and casual criticism, these societies have a great variety of practices – usually institutionalised, standardised and hedged about with conventions so as to prevent them getting out of hand – whose aim is to criticise, shame or ridicule persons suspected of committing delicts or in some cases to publicise the delict and to discover its perpetrator. An example of both is given by the Hopi's use of a sort of public crier, who chants grievances in a standardised manner from a rooftop, expressing regret that such things should be done (thereby underlining Hopi norms) and reprimanding the offender or calling on the pueblo for help in identifying him.[55] The use of ridicule among the Eskimo, especially in the form of the 'song duel', is well known. Among those of the Canadian Northwest Territories, for example, derision is used '(a) constantly in daily intercourse; (b) in spontaneously sung lampoons during common gatherings in the large winter festival house; and (c) in formal "song-duels" in the same situation'.[56] In these duels, contestants 'sing' before an amused and applauding audience which acts as arbitrator, and with sarcasm, irony and wit accuse one another of 'incest, bestiality, murder, avarice, adultery, failure at hunting, being henpecked, lack of manly strength'. These duels serve to keep the whole community informed about its members' behaviour (and indeed good performance in song duels *requires* that a man keep himself well-informed about others) as well as reiterating and underlining social norms.

An elaborate example of institutionalised public shaming is the system of competitive food exchanges on Goodenough Island (off Papua) described by Michael Young in his *Fighting with Food*.[57] Sorcery accusations (to be discussed below) are a potent instrument of social control in this Melanesian society; harangues delivered from a house-top on a dark night publicise delicts to most of the village with the intention of shaming an unknown offender and may result in the exile of a named offender; and the clans (between which there is imperfect exogamy) are crosscut by ties of kinship, by 'eating companion-ships' (food is very important to these people), and by traditional food-giving partnerships (*fofofo*). But according to Young the most important instrument of order in this acephalous society is the *abutu* or 'food-giving-to-shame'. An *abutu* is triggered by a

[55] R. A. Black, 'Hopi grievance chants: a mechanism of social control', in D. Hymes and W. E. Brittle, eds., *Studies in Southwestern Ethnolinguistics* (The Hague: Mouton, 1967).
[56] Gluckman, *Politics, Law and Ritual*, p. 304.
[57] Michael W. Young, *Fighting with Food* (Cambridge: Cambridge University Press, 1971).

delict and takes place about once a year between hostile factions of the village, less frequently between villages. Each side attempts to shame the other by giving it more and better food (domestic pigs, taro, bananas and especially yams) than it is able to pay back simultaneously. The principals, who initiate the *abutu*, do not retain this food; it must be redistributed among their respective *fofofo*, who also make speeches at the *abutu* on behalf of the principals. Young concludes that, although this practice may in a limited sense be redressive and that it may sometimes compound problems of social control rather than solve them, the threat of *abutu* is nevertheless seen by the natives as a very real sanction and it evidently serves effectively to shame offenders by publicising delicts (and shame is a well-developed emotion in this society) as well as bringing about a *détente* through the temporary mutual exhaustion of resources by the village's political factions.

The final group of social controls which I shall consider consists of threats of sorcery and accusations of witchcraft and of supernatural sanctions. Witchcraft beliefs are not found universally (and where accusations are made they are not a sanction of first resort). It appears that witchcraft beliefs are less likely to be found where social relations are well-defined, where social interaction is not intensive and especially where people can move away from each other easily. Such beliefs are not, for example, found among the Mbuti pygmies of the Congo and are unimportant among the Nuer.[58] Where beliefs in witchcraft do exist, a person who suffers some misfortune may accuse

---

[58] See Mary Douglas, ed., *Witchcraft Accusations and Confessions* (London: Tavistock, 1970), editor's Introduction, p. xxxiii, and ch. 13 by Godfrey Lienhardt on 'The situation of death: an aspect of Anuak philosophy'; and Paul Baxter, 'Absence makes the heart grow fonder; some suggestions why witchcraft accusations are rare among East African pastoralists', in Max Gluckman, ed., *The Allocation of Responsibility* (Manchester: Manchester University Press, 1972).

another individual of working witchcraft against him or consult a diviner or oracle to discover the witch, and the individual accused is invariably a personal enemy and one already known for his anti-social conduct. (In acephalous societies – always egalitarian – accusations may be made against anyone who acquires much more than others or who becomes eminent. I return to this in Chapter 3.) The punishment meted out varies from the accused's identity being publicised by gossip to ostracism or death. This deters the individual from anti-social behaviour and encourages cooperativeness and generosity and the performance of obligations by creating both a fear of being accused of working witchcraft and a fear of being bewitched by someone he would displease.[59]

Fear of the misfortune and adversity meted out as punishment by a variety of spirits and deities is an important and widespread instrument of social control. In many societies, certain spirits are thought to be angered by hostile relations between kinsmen or between members of the same local community. In parts of Africa, for example, the earth is venerated and the greatest sacrilege against it is to spill blood in fighting.[60] Often, actions are religiously sanctioned which, though they do not contribute directly to social order (in the narrow senses discussed above), may contribute indirectly by helping to maintain other practices or structures which play a role in the maintenance of order (and generally they contribute to social order in the wider senses). Thus, ancestral spirits punish people for defaulting on their obligations to kinsmen (as well as for failing to worship the ancestral spirits themselves); and *kwoth*, the central deity of the Nuer, is offended by, amongst other things, incest.

[59] See generally Gluckman, *Politics, Law and Ritual*, ch. 6; and Guy E. Swanson, *The Birth of the Gods* (Ann Arbor: Michigan University Press, 1960), ch. 8.
[60] See for example M. Fortes, 'The political system of the Tallensi of the Northern Territories of the Gold Coast', in M. Fortes and E. E. Evans-Pritchard, eds., *African Political Systems* (London: Oxford University Press, 1940).

Finally, it is worth noting that although the authorities and leaders of stateless societies lack power, the positions they occupy often have a religious and mythical warrant; they are to some degree sanctified. In view of the role these authorities play in preventing and settling disputes directly and in upholding other institutions and practices which I have already discussed, such sanctity doubtless enhances the contribution they make to the maintenance of order.[61]

When we turn from primitive stateless societies to peasant societies, we find essentially that, with certain qualifications and a redistribution of emphasis, the means by which social order is maintained are the same. Having described these in some detail for the primitive societies, I shall simply summarise here very briefly the qualifications that have to be made in the case of peasant communities, which, as I noted in Section 1.5, are internally only quasi-anarchic and vary considerably in the degree to which they possess the three core attributes of community.

Reciprocity and the threat of the withdrawal of reciprocal aid (and of ostracism and expulsion) are of great importance in peasant communities of the closed corporate kind, as they are in primitive anarchies. Their importance is diminished in the 'open' peasant communities, because there is less economic interdependence between members of the community and greater dependence of its members on outsiders. The threat of 'self-help' retaliation, including feuding, is found in peasant communities, but much less commonly than in primitive societies, precisely because the peasant community is an integral part of a society with a state, and is subject to some

---

[61] Roy A. Rapoport has claimed (a little exaggeratedly, I think) that sanctity is a functional equivalent of political power and steadily diminishes with the growth of centralised power. 'The sacred in human evolution', *Annual Review of Ecology and Systematics*, 2 (1971), 23–44.

extent to the laws and the power of lord and state. It is this feature of social control which the state (in part by definition) first displaces. 'The pressure of public opinion' – shaming, ridiculing, gossiping, and so on – seems to play a central role in maintaining order in every peasant community. Threats of witchcraft accusations and of supernatural sanctions are important in many peasant societies, but in some communities (including some closed corporate communities) supernatural sanctions do not seem to be very much feared and witchcraft is unimportant.

Intentional communities are, like peasant communities, in general quasi-anarchic internally but embedded in a society with a state. As in peasant communities, the social controls they use are therefore supplementary to those exercised by the state, though the state may have little penetration in these communities and recourse to its sanctions is often avoided where possible. Partly because they are subject to a state and partly because in almost every case their members are opposed to the use of violence, the threat of 'self-help' retaliation is rarely encountered, at least in the American and English intentional communities of the nineteenth and twentieth centuries. In the religious communities, supernatural sanctions, ceremonial and ritual played a part in maintaining order, though in most cases a small one; and witchcraft was not practised. Controls based on the sanctions of approval and disapproval played the most important role in all these communities. These controls are explicitly recognised and used in institutionalised public criticism, shaming and ridiculing devices in the 'utopian' communities. In the modern secular communes, however, such devices are rare, and in most cases their members would not approve of them; nevertheless informal and un-organised gossip and signs of approval and disapproval conveyed in everyday interaction play an important part, and it is hard to see how it could be otherwise among people living, eating and often working together in small groups. Ostracism and expulsion are of course practised, but the threat of them, especially expulsion, cannot have the powerful deterrent effect which they have in primitive communities, for if a person becomes unpopular and chooses to leave or if he or she is expelled, it is a less serious matter. Finally, in nearly all intentional communities, of both utopian and secular types, the threat of withdrawal of reciprocal aid is not an important means of social control. The chief reason for this is that in most of these communities there is approximately equal access to communal property and equal availability of collectively produced goods (especially food) and services, usually subject to everyone's needs first being satisfied, and, crucially, free access and availability are not denied those who do not exchange their labour reciprocally with the rest of the community and do not do their part in producing these goods and services. This principle of distribution creates its own free rider problem and failure to solve it is a main cause of the collapse of these communities; I shall have more to say about it in the next chapter.

I have given here only a very brief summary of the similarities and differences between the social controls of the primitive anarchies and those found (in addition to such controls as the state exercises) in peasant and intentional communities. This summary will be filled out with some illustrations in Section 3.2 where I shall discuss the use of these same controls to contain the development of inequality.

2.5 Community and stateless social order

There are, then, four principal groups of social controls which are used to maintain social order in the primitive stateless societies and to a lesser extent also in quasi-anarchic peasant and intentional communities where they are supplemented by controls associated with the state. The principal types of social controls are (i) the threat of 'self-help' retaliation, (ii) the offer of reciprocity and the threat of its withdrawal, (iii) the use of the sanctions of approval and disapproval, the latter especially *via* gossip, ridicule and shaming, and (iv) the threat of witchcraft accusations and of supernatural sanctions. Controls based on supernatural sanctions obviously differ from the rest since, although they are a product of a community's beliefs, the sanctions are not entirely at the disposal of the community's members. With the exception of the use of supernatural sanctions, all four types of social control characteristic of anarchies can be effective only in groups which are relatively small and have little turnover in their memberships. The practice of reciprocity is unlikely to flourish (and therefore the threat of its withdrawal cannot be an important social control) where people do not have *stable* relations with *known* individuals – individuals who are expected to remain in the group and to be able therefore to reciprocate aid. Like reciprocity, 'self-help' retaliation *can* be practised in large and mobile societies but is clearly more difficult to pursue in such societies than in smaller and more stable ones. The same is evidently true of the use of gossip and of ridiculing and shaming devices. These operate more effectively on an individual if he is known to all or most of the community, if his delicts or his defaulting on reciprocal giving become known to virtually everyone in his world, if he cannot escape into anonymity and must continue to live for the rest of his life with the same small set of people (or with a breakaway subset of them in the case of fission: see below). Finally, the threat of witchcraft accusations can also contribute more effectively to the maintenance of social order in small, stable groups since, like ridiculing and shaming, their use depends critically both on people being well-informed about each other's behaviour and on the prospect of having to live (if allowed to live) among the same group of familiar people with the reputation resulting from a successful witchcraft accusation.

The primitive stateless communities discussed in the preceding section are of course small and very stable. Even where there is population growth, a community remains small by breaking up whenever it has grown too large for its members to work local land: a part of the community splits off and establishes itself on new land. This process of *fissioning* (which I shall have more to say about in Section 3.3 on the origins of the state) is a normal part of the life of stateless societies. Merely by helping to ensure that communities remain small, it contributes indirectly to the maintenance of social order. But fissioning may also occur when there is persistent internal conflict, especially where population densities are low and unused productive land is available, and even more readily among gatherers and hunters and shifting cultivators who have negligible property and minimal sunk investments in whatever land they are using. In this case, the people who move away may be able to join kinsmen elsewhere and thus gain support and protection.[62]

Now if community is characterised (as it was in Section 1.4) by shared values and beliefs, direct and many-sided relations, and the practice of reciprocity, then communities must be small and stable, for in a large group with changing membership few relations between individuals can be direct and many-sided and reciprocity cannot flourish on a wide scale. But smallness and stability do not entail community. A small set of individuals with fairly stable membership *need* not have many values and beliefs in common, or deal with each other directly and as rounded individuals rather than as specialists, or practise reciprocity amongst themselves. I have argued that smallness and stability are necessary conditions for the social controls

---

[62] For an example of fission of this kind, see Jack Stauder, 'Anarchy and ecology: political society among the Majangir', *Southwestern Journal of Anthropology*, 28 (1972), 153–68.

characteristic of anarchies to be effective. But they are clearly not sufficient, since, in the first place, one of the attributes of community, reciprocity, must be practised if the threat of its withdrawal is to be an effective control. Furthermore, the effectiveness of gossip, ridicule and shaming in maintaining social order depends not only on smallness and stability but on the other two features of community – shared beliefs and values and direct many-sided relations; for a person who does not deal directly with those around him or has only one-sided or specialised relations with some of them, and has few values and beliefs in common with them, is unlikely to be very sensitive to their criticism. Thus the two most important means of maintaining social order in stateless societies – those based on reciprocity and on approval and disapproval – together depend on community for their effectiveness.

Let us recall the argument about public goods and group size which was summarised in the first section of this chapter. It is that public goods are more likely to be provided, or provided in optimal amounts, by the members of *small* publics than by those of large ones. In the static analysis given by Olson, this is chiefly because the larger the public, the smaller the benefit which accrues to any individual member from the additional amount of the public good provided out of his contribution, so that in a relatively large group this benefit is likely to be exceeded by the cost to him of making the contribution, whereas in a relatively small group this is less likely to be the case. But a more realistic dynamic analysis leads to a similar conclusion, for it shows (what is intuitively nearly obvious) that the only rational cooperation is *conditional* cooperation whereby an individual contributes if and only if enough others contribute, and such conditional cooperation is possible only in a relatively small public in which people have contact with and can observe the behaviour of many of their fellows and which has a fairly stable membership. Now we have just seen that these same conditions – smallness and stability – are also necessary conditions for the methods of social control characteristic of anarchies to be effective. However, the size at which it would be rational for the members of a group to provide themselves with a public good like social order would generally be smaller than the range of sizes necessary for these methods to function. In other words, in *very* small publics, no 'selective incentives' or controls are needed: it is rational to cooperate voluntarily in the production of the public good of social order; but in larger publics, controls of some kind – *some* means of getting people to do things they otherwise would not do – are necessary if social order is to be maintained. The methods which are used by societies without a state are effective only in small and stable communities.

3

Equality in anarchy

3.1 Is equality unstable in anarchy?

The argument of the previous chapter is, very roughly, that anarchy requires community, for only in community can social order be maintained without the state. Community in turn clearly requires a measure of economic equality – a rough equality of basic material conditions – for as the gap increases between rich and poor, so their values diverge, relations between them are likely to become less direct and many-sided, and the sense of interdependence which supports a system of (generalised and near generalised) reciprocity is weakened. The economic equality that is a condition of community need be far from perfect: only gross inequality undermines community.

But according to a traditional argument, associated especially with writers of a liberal persuasion, economic equality or approximate equality would not survive for long in the absence of the state. An egalitarian distribution (or any other distribution) of resources would soon be disrupted, as individuals appropriated previously unowned resources or gave away, stole and above all exchanged resources in the absence of any restraint or rectification by the state. If this is so, and if anarchy is possible only in community while community is incompatible with inequality, then anarchy does not appear to be viable. I propose in this chapter to show that this is not so: to defend the view that an approximate economic equality *can* be maintained in the absence of the state – but only in community. On my account, then, community needs equality and at the same time provides conditions in which it can survive. The distribution of resources is derivative and instrumental, and I must emphasise that I neither assume nor argue that equality – any sort of equality – is in itself an end or ideal. What is central to my argument in this book is the quality of relations between people. Economic equality is important but only because it is a necessary (though not of course sufficient) condition of community.

Since economic or material equality would soon be disturbed by the voluntary actions of individuals, it follows, according to the argument I shall oppose, that even if an approximate equality were achieved, it could be maintained only by continuous interference by the state in people's lives. This, it is then argued, is undesirable because it would restrict individual liberty (which in this context is the absence of deliberate interference in the individual's choice of action by others using force or coercion), or it would violate individual rights (to use and dispose of legitimately acquired property as one sees fit). If rights are held to be inviolable come what may, then economic equality must be sacrificed. If liberty has priority, if not a single individual's liberty may be restricted – even if doing so would increase the liberty of many others or would further other widely valued aims – then redistributive state interference cannot be countenanced.

A range of liberals, 'libertarians' and anarcho-capitalists subscribe to this old argument. F. A. Hayek and Robert Nozick are two well-known exponents. In *The Mirage of Social Justice* Hayek writes that 'While an equality of rights under limited government is possible and an essential condition of individual freedom, a claim for equality of material position can be met only by a government with totalitarian powers.'[1] Nozick, in

---

[1] Friedrich A. Hayek, *Law, Legislation and Liberty*, vol. 2: *The Mirage of Social Justice* (Chicago: University of Chicago Press, 1976), p. 83.

Anarchy, State and Utopia, rejects not only egalitarian principles of distribution but all distributive principles which are patterned or unhistorical or both. A principle is *patterned* 'if it specifies that a distribution is to vary along with some natural dimension, weighted sum of dimensions, or lexicographic ordering of dimensions'.[2] Most of the standard principles of distributive justice are patterned: to each according to his needs, to each according to his contribution, and so on. *Historical* principles 'hold that past circumstances or actions of people can create differential entitlements or differential deserts to things': the justice of a distribution depends on how it came about. Both patterned and unpatterned principles may be historical or unhistorical. 'To each according to how hard she has worked' is a patterned historical principle. 'To each according to IQ' and 'to each according to sex' are patterned but unhistorical. An example of a distributive principle which is neither patterned nor historical is one requiring only that the distribution is one that maximises social welfare.

To all three types of principle Nozick objects. He objects to them because their application results in the violation of individual rights which, he assumes, are inviolable side constraints and include the right to private property. Think of your favourite distribution, he says, a distribution (call it D1) in which, we assume for the sake of argument, everyone is entitled to their holdings. Perhaps the distribution gives everyone an equal share. Then if some people voluntarily exchanged some of their holdings or even merely made gifts to others, this favoured distribution would be transformed into a new one (D2) which would not in general conform to the favoured principle. In Nozick's own notorious example, an outstanding basketball player, Wilt Chamberlain, is offered by some team a payment of 25¢ out of the price of every home game admission ticket:

[2] Nozick, *Anarchy, State and Utopia*, p. 156.

The season starts, and people cheerfully attend his team's games; they buy their tickets, each time dropping a separate twenty-five cents of their admission price into a special box with Chamberlain's name on it. They are excited about seeing him play; it is worth the total admission price to them. Let us suppose that in one season one million persons attend his home games, and Wilt Chamberlain winds up with $250,000, a much larger sum than the average income and larger even than anyone else has. Is he entitled to this income? Is this new distribution D2, unjust? If so, why? There is *no* question about whether each of the people was entitled to the control over the resources they held in D1; because that was the distribution (your favorite) that (for the purposes of argument) we assumed was acceptable. Each of these persons *chose* to give twenty-five cents of their money to Chamberlain. They could have spent it on going to the movies, or on candy bars, or on copies of *Dissent* magazine, or of *Monthly Review*. But they all, at least one million of them, converged on giving it to Wilt Chamberlain in exchange for watching him play basketball. If D1 was a just distribution, and people voluntarily moved from it to D2, transferring parts of their shares they were given under D1 (what was it for if not to do something with?), isn't D2 also just? If the people were entitled to dispose of the resources to which they were entitled (under D1), didn't this include their being entitled to give it to, or exchange it with, Wilt Chamberlain? Can anyone else complain on grounds of justice? Each other person already has his legitimate share under D1. Under D1, there is nothing that anyone has that anyone else has a claim of justice against. After someone transfers something to Wilt Chamberlain, third parties *still* have their legitimate shares; *their* shares are not changed.[3]

The favoured pattern D1, any pattern, says Nozick, could not be maintained without continual or periodical interference to stop people 'voluntarily' transferring resources as they see fit or to take from them resources others have voluntarily transferred to them. 'Liberty upsets patterns' and maintaining patterns violates rights and limits liberty. Nozick's own 'entitlement theory' of justice is unpatterned and historical. It deems a distribution just if every individual is entitled to his or her holdings under the distribution and an individual is entitled to a holding if it results from 'just acquisition' or voluntary transfers

---

[3] *Anarchy, State and Utopia*, p. 161.

(gifts or voluntary exchanges) between individuals entitled to their holdings. (The principle of just acquisition is a modified version of Locke's idea that one becomes entitled to previously unowned resources by mixing one's labour with them.)[4]

Of the many objections that can be lodged against Nozick's entitlement theory and his rejection of the alternatives, I want to draw attention here to two or three which bear on my own arguments. First, even if the Lockean starting point (that individuals have rights) is accepted and it is accepted that non-violation of these is a side constraint on action, it has still to be shown that these rights include full 'capitalist' rights to private property, entitling an individual (provided others' rights are not violated) to control and use any amount of any sort of resource in any way whatsoever.[5] Nozick does not provide such a demonstration but his argument depends on property rights being of this sort, as can be seen in the Wilt Chamberlain story quoted earlier. A part of any appeal this story may have is that justice in transfer requires the transfers to be *voluntary*. Nozick admits that other people's actions may restrict the range of options available to an individual, but in his view such restriction only makes the resulting actions of that individual non-voluntary if the others did not have a right to act as they did (even if they restrict the individual's choice to two extremely unattractive options).[6] This, I submit, is an arbitrary and bizarre stipulative definition. The effects on the individual's choice conditions are the same whether the others act within their rights or not.

Now what is supposed by Nozick to make a distribution just is that (assuming away any problems to do with original

[4] *Anarchy, State and Utopia*, pp. 174–82.
[5] See the discussion of this point in Thomas Nagel, 'Libertarianism without foundations', *Yale Law Journal*, 85 (1975), 136–49; Onora O'Neill, 'Nozick's entitlements', *Inquiry*, 19 (1976), 468–81; and Cheyney C. Ryan, 'Yours, mine and ours: property rights and individual liberty', *Ethics*, 87 (1976–7), 126–41.
[6] *Anarchy, State and Utopia*, pp. 262–5.

acquisition) it was brought about voluntarily, by agreement, by consent. But in fact *it* – the distribution – was *not* brought about in this way. All that a participating individual agrees to, engages in voluntarily, are the transactions he makes with others. An individual does not agree to a new distribution resulting from the transactions of everybody or of a large number of people. In *some* cases he could perhaps predict roughly what the distribution would become if many others act as he does (give Wilt Chamberlain 25¢ each week, for example), but if he doesn't like that outcome, he is confronted with a free rider problem. (He would prefer everyone else not to contribute to the enrichment of Wilt Chamberlain to everybody contributing, but neither making nor withholding *his* contribution has much effect on the distribution of wealth, so he'd prefer to contribute no matter how many others do.)

One upshot of the aggregate of transfers may be that one or more individuals (like Wilt Chamberlain) acquire wealth sufficient to give them considerable power over others. In a modern industrial society, where wealth and power are already very unequally distributed, few people might care that someone like Wilt Chamberlain joins the rich. But, as G. A. Cohen has pointed out, this may not be so in a society where wealth and power are more or less equally distributed. 'Human nature' in such a society may very well be such that people will choose to act in ways which maintain the equal distribution. This scenario and a Nozickean scenario in which 'voluntary' transfers soon disrupt an egalitarian distribution *both* rest on their own conceptions of human nature.[7] On one view, maintaining equality is problematic and is not easily squared with liberty, but on the other view this is not so.

In fact, there have been societies whose members did value

[7] G. A. Cohen, 'Robert Nozick and Wilt Chamberlain: how patterns preserve liberty', in J. Arthur and W. H. Shaw, eds., *Justice and Economic Distribution* (Englewood Cliffs, NJ: Prentice-Hall, 1978).

equality, or at least acted so as to maintain an approximate equality. And they acted in this way (in some cases for millennia) without any interference by the state, indeed in the total absence of the state. They refrained from doing some of the things which would have led to gross inequalities and they redistributed resources from the temporarily rich to those temporarily in need. But it would be wrong to describe their actions as 'voluntary'. There were always positive and negative sanctions, some of them dire, tacitly threatened by the community against a potential non-participant in these equalising or levelling practices. I do not know of a single society of which it could be reasonably said that equality, even a very rough equality, is maintained voluntarily. The growth of economic inequality had to be contained by controls (which I shall discuss in the following section) involving tacit threats and offers even in societies where individuals had severely restricted property rights – even where, for example, the legal ownership of important resources was vested in collectives (such as lineages, or clans, or village communities) to which the conditional use-rights of individuals or households were subject – though of course collective ownership does slow down the development of inequality between individuals by limiting what can be privately accumulated and by removing a source of private incentive to produce more. It is true that all the experience of primitive and peasant communities, intentional communities, and collectives and communes in 'socialist' societies – even those whose members have grown up and have been well socialised in the community – does not *prove* that there can never be societies where 'human nature', appropriately socialised, will be such that equality is maintained voluntarily; but certainly this evidence gives no grounds for optimism.

Economic equality, then, is unlikely to last indefinitely without *some* counteracting influence, some means of getting people to do things they would otherwise not do.[8] But the counteracting influence which maintains the pattern need not be the state (as Nozick's critics and others tend to assume). Just as social order can be maintained without the state, so an approximate economic equality can be (and in fact was) maintained in stateless societies. Of course, the means of maintaining equality may, like the redistributive state, curtail some people's liberty. But that in itself would not be a sufficient reason to reject them (and to accept the resulting inequality), just as it is not a sufficient reason to reject the redistributive state. (I shall take up this question in the chapter on liberty.) The thesis I shall develop in the following section is that in the absence of a strong state the emergence and development of gross inequalities *can* be contained, but only in the small community; or, to put it another way, community is a necessary condition for the maintenance of an approximate equality (*within* the community; the problem of inequality *between* communities is put aside here – I shall return to it briefly (but not solve it) in Chapter 5).

I am interested here only in how economic equality fares in anarchy, and this because such equality is a necessary condition for relations between people to be those characteristic of community. Economic equality is not the only kind of equality required for community. A rough equality of *participation* in collective decision-making and a rough equality in the *exercise of power* are also required. An extensive inequality of participation is inconsistent with the condition that relations between

---

[8] So far as I can see this is true of *any* distributive pattern – including the 'income-fair' allocation and the less impractical 'wealth-fair' allocation considered by Hal R. Varian in 'Equity, envy and efficiency', *Journal of Economic Theory*, 9 (1974), 63–91, and 'Distributive justice, welfare economics and the theory of fairness', *Philosophy and Public Affairs*, 4 (1974–5), 223–47. These two allocations are not upset by trading – but only if it is trading in a competitive market. All transfers outside the market, including gifts and bequests, would have to be prevented, and, to bring about a wealth-fair allocation, wealth has to be equalised among the members of each new generation. Clearly, a great deal of control would be needed to maintain this distribution.

people are direct and many-sided, for in the matters in which there is not full participation by everyone there is effectively mediation between people: problems and disputes are solved not by the parties involved dealing directly with each other but by those who participate. 'The more a human group lets itself be represented in the management of its common affairs... the less communal life there is in it and the more impoverished it becomes as a community.'[9]

Gross asymmetries in the exercise of power (in the sense indicated in Section 1.3) also undermine community: reciprocity is unlikely to flourish and relations are unlikely to remain direct and many-sided. Anything which is valued is a potential base for the exercise of power. Two such bases are economic or material resources and control of force. An equal distribution of each of these two things does not entail an equal distribution of power, because there may be other valued things (for example: information, or a person's good opinion) which are unequally distributed and because whether an individual has power over another depends on their preferences as well as their resources. But economic resources and the control of force are the two most important bases for the exercise of power, and equality in their distribution would go a long way to ensuring that there is a rough overall equality in the exercise of power.

Since my concern here is with how equality fares in *anarchies*, the question is therefore whether *economic* equality can survive, for in an anarchy (as I argued in Section 1.2) there is minimal concentration of force and division of political labour, hence an approximate equality of the control of force and participation.

The most apparent reason why the growth of economic inequality would be inhibited in a community is that most people, even if they were not dealing with friends, would feel

---

[9] Buber, *Paths in Utopia*, p. 133.

uncomfortable if they were stingy towards or took advantage of others whom they must continue to live with, meeting them frequently and dealing with them face-to-face. In a (small, stable) community such behaviour – exploitative behaviour, ambitious striving for eminence or advantage, taking advantage of others' kindness, not reciprocating aid – seems inappropriate and causes embarrassment and discomfort. But (as will be clear from the discussion in the next section) such feelings would not alone suffice to inhibit the growth of inequality. These embarrassed and uncomfortable feelings are in fact a kind of automatic *sanction* and what is involved here is a special case of social control based on shame and the sense of guilt. Social controls are necessary if equality is to survive in anarchy and my argument in the next section – an extension of the argument in the last chapter – is that non-governmental controls can contain the development of inequality only in the small and stable community.

3.2 *The control of inequality in stateless societies*

As in Chapter 2, I approach this question by looking in the first place at how an approximate equality is or was in fact maintained in stateless and quasi-stateless societies. Again, the relevant cases are of four sorts: (1) primitive stateless societies, divided into (1a) acephalous societies proper and (1b) redistributive systems (chiefdoms and big-man systems); (2) peasant communities, especially those of the 'closed corporate' variety; and (3) intentional communities, including the utopian communities of the nineteenth and twentieth centuries and Israeli *kibbutzim* and *shitufim*.

How then is the development of inequality restrained in societies of these kinds? I look first at those arrangements and practices in them which have levelling or equalising tendencies and then at the social controls which ensure the individual behaviour necessary to maintain these arrangements and practices.

Any emergence or growth of inequality in primitive societies – especially in the strictly acephalous societies but to a lesser extent also in the chiefdoms and in the intermediate big-man systems – has in the first place to contend with (or at any rate work itself out within the structure of) the 'domestic mode of production' (or DMP). The central features of the DMP, as described by Marshall Sahlins, are as follows. 'The household as such is charged with production, with the deployment and use of labor-power, with the determination of the economic objective. Its own inner relations, as between husband and wife, parent and child, are the principal relations of production in society.'[10] The principal form of economic specialisation or division of labour is based on sex. Within the household there is pooling of goods and services – a 'communism in living' which gives to every member roughly according to his or her needs regardless of contribution. Production is for use, for the family's livelihood, not for profit (which does not mean that households are self-sufficient; but when they exchange, that too is to provide for their needs). The technology used by these nearly autonomous domestic units of limited production for use is appropriately simple: small-scale, made and used by every family and fully under its members' control. The 'economy' is underproductive: resources are not fully used (they could support a larger population), nor is labour-power. In particular, production in these societies conforms very roughly to 'Chayanov's rule', according to which the productive intensity of a household varies inversely with its productive capacity, that is to say, the greater the ratio of workers to consumers in the household, the less each member works.[11] There are important

[10] Sahlins, *Stone Age Economics*, pp. 76–7.
[11] See A. V. Chayanov, *The Theory of Peasant Economy* (Homewood, Ill.: Richard D. Irwin, 1966) and Sahlins, *Stone Age Economics*, chs. 2 and 3. Chayanov

exceptions to this rule and one effect of them should be noted here for its levelling tendency: kinship relations between households may in part counteract the working of Chayanov's rule, for they may oblige workers from households endowed with a high worker/consumer ratio to work more than the norm indicated by the rule in order to help related households with a low ratio.

What, finally, of ownership of and access to resources in the DMP? The most important resource is land. In hunting and gathering societies, although each band typically confines itself mainly to a traditional territory, its members usually do not think of themselves as having an *exclusive* right to the territory (or to the game on it): it is open to other bands. Scarcer resources – like the water-holes and fertile areas with the edible plants – may be associated more definitely and more exclusively with each band. In tribal societies of cultivators, 'ownership' of land is vested in lineages or clans or chiefs; but although the household does not exclusively own land, it always has access to it. It has a conditional usufruct, which may be overridden; the chief or the corporate lineage may deny its members the use of a piece of land if they are not making proper use of it or are failing in their obligations to others. Usually, too, the household owns domesticated animals, the crops it has produced and any other food it has gathered or killed. In both kinds of society there is family or individual ownership of houses and of clothes, utensils, tools and weapons: all these things can typically be easily and freely replaced, for there is unlimited access to the necessary raw materials.

It will be evident from this sketch of the DMP that it is not a promising framework for the growth of gross inequality. The right of each household to enjoy either unrestricted access to basic resources or use of a portion of them (even though this

formulated this rule on the basis of evidence from Russian peasant production just before the Revolution.

use-right is conditional and coexists with corporate 'over-rights') inhibits the emergence of a class of landless families dependent on those with exclusive control of these resources. More importantly each household has limited objectives: it is a 'satisficer', not a maximiser. Having provided for its needs, it goes no further. Those families which would find it easiest to produce more – those with a favourable worker/consumer ratio – do not do so: in other words Chayanov's rule has a levelling tendency. Where the better-placed families produce above the Chayanov norm, it is in order to assist those less favourably placed; and this also has a levelling tendency (one I shall return to below). Even if a family *did* produce more than it could use, there is often nothing useful it could do with the surplus (it cannot be stored, for the techniques are not known, and it cannot be sold) except to give it away.

The domestic mode of production is of course an ideal type. While it is a fair characterisation of production in the acephalous primitive societies, chiefdoms and big-man systems conform to it only approximately: in particular, Chayanov's rule begins to break down, production is intensified, and there may be some division of labour beyond that between man and woman. Associated with these modifications of the DMP there are also important differences, as we move from strictly egalitarian societies to chiefdoms, in the structure of reciprocities. There are two basic structures. On the one hand, the structure of reciprocities is unmediated and symmetric, with movement of goods directly between any two members of the community. On the other hand, the structure is mediated or centralised, with movement of goods towards a centre (a big man or chief) and then outwards. The second type is usually called *redistributive*; but remains a structure of reciprocities. In both cases the structure is made up of dyadic exchanges and these can in principle be anywhere on the spectrum of reciprocities described in Chapter 1. In practice they tend in both cases towards the generalised end of the spectrum – generalised among close kin (and therefore also within the local community) and generalised or nearly so between the people and their big-man or chief.

In hunting and gathering societies the spoils of hunting, especially the large game, are shared out with close kin within the band (possibly the whole band) or camp or local group, and there is more balanced reciprocity with more distant kin within the camp or band or in other local groups.[12] The Nuer, to take a well-known acephalous tribal example, practise generalised reciprocity within hamlets and cattle camps, but there is little exchange between the more inclusive tribal sectors.[13]

In redistributive systems the chief has a customary right to collect dues – a levy on the produce of the community – and is under customary obligation to use it generously for the benefit of his people, by 'subsidizing religious ceremony, social pageantry, or war; underwriting craft production, trade, the construction of technical apparatus and of public and religious edifices; redistributing diverse local products; hospitality and succor of the community (in severalty and in general) during shortage'.[14]

---

[12] For example, see Lorna Marshall, 'Sharing, talking and giving'; Lee, The !Kung San; Robert F. Spencer, The North Alaskan Eskimo: A Study in Ecology and Society, Smithsonian Institution Bureau of American Ethnology Bulletin 171 (Washington, DC: US Government Printing Office, 1959); Colin Turnbull, The Forest People (London: Jonathan Cape, 1961); and A. R. Radcliffe-Brown, The Andaman Islanders (Cambridge: Cambridge University Press, 1922).

[13] E. E. Evans-Pritchard, The Nuer.

[14] Sahlins, Stone Age Economics, p. 190. For accounts of reciprocity and redistribution in big-man systems, see Douglas Oliver, A Solomon Island Society (Cambridge, Mass.: Harvard University Press, 1955); Marie Reay, The Kuma; and Leopold Pospisil, Kapauku Papuans and their Law, Yale University Publications in Anthropology no. 54 (New Haven, Conn.: Yale University Press, 1958). Excellent accounts of redistribution in chiefdoms are to be found in Bronislaw Malinowski, Argonauts of the Western Pacific (London: Routledge and Kegan Paul, 1922); Raymond Firth, We, the Tikopia (London: Allen and Unwin, 1936) and Economics of the New Zealand Maori, 2nd edition (Wellington, New Zealand: R. E. Owen, Government Printer, 1959); and Audrey Richards, Land, Labour and Diet in Northern Rhodesia, 2nd edition (London: Oxford University Press, 1961). On Melanesian and Polynesian redistributive systems generally, see Marshall Sahlins, 'Poor man, rich man, big-man, chief: political types in Melanesia and Polynesia', Comparative Studies in Society and History, 5 (1963), 285–303.

A feature shared by all these structures of reciprocity is that generalised reciprocity is generally operated in favour of those in need: those (temporarily) better-off are expected to share with or give to the needy. 'Kinsmen must assist one another, and if one has a surplus of a good thing he must share it with his neighbours. Consequently no Nuer ever has a surplus.'[15]

In the acephalous societies this bias in the practice of generalised reciprocity, set in the context of the domestic mode of production (especially the unimpeded access of all families to land and to the resources necessary for building, tool-making, etc.), ensures a high degree of equality of economic position. And more generally there is an approximate equality of power. For although there are individuals with prestige and authority, their recommendations cannot be backed by credible threats. Prestige is based on personal qualities. A man acquires a reputation as a successful hunter or as a skilled mediator; he is therefore respected and his advice heeded – but only in the matter of hunting or dispute settlement. He exercises authority. And if occasionally an individual combines several excellences, he may have something of the position of a charismatic leader – but again with no power. So, there is in these acephalous societies a limited inequality of prestige. There are also inequalities based on sex and age (as there are, so far as I know, in every society). Men and women do different jobs (for example, in hunting and gathering societies usually the men hunt, the women gather), and adult males tend to do the very limited amount of collective decision-making, in which elders tend to have more influence. In most respects, though, the acephalous societies are fundamentally egalitarian, certainly more equal than any other sort of society (with the exceptions of a few intentional 'utopian' communities – but these are only part-societies).

[15] Evans-Pritchard, *The Nuer*, p. 183.

The effect of reciprocities on inequality in the redistributive systems is a little more complicated. Let us recall that the chiefdoms, which are intermediate between acephalous societies and true states, have hierarchies of formal, hereditary statuses, with strong theocratic and divinely sanctioned leadership which organises the redistribution of produce, religious ceremonies, festivities, war, public building works, and so on. There is, in other words, considerable inequality of prestige, authority and participation. Nevertheless the chiefs have no more power, in the sense I have been using this word, than other individuals, and they have no control of concentrated force. They may be respected and obeyed; but not because of an ability to make credible threats or to wield concentrated force. Most often a chief's prestige is in large measure dependent on his generosity; he is under a strong obligation to use what he has received in the service of his people (to make gifts, provision feasts, finance public works, etc.). The result in many cases is that the chief gives as much as, and at times more than, he is given; so that over time his wealth is no greater than that of commoners or is so only temporarily. A considerable inequality of prestige and participation, then, is built on a generosity which periodically levels the distribution of economic resources.

Intermediate between the basically egalitarian acephalous societies and the chiefdoms are the big-man systems. A big man at first attracts followers because he possesses qualities of the sort that make charismatic leaders in acephalous societies, and then builds and maintains a position of leadership through generous giving, a position with greater prestige than that of leaders in acephalous societies. Not only does the big man, like the chief, lack power and the control of concentrated force, but his position tends to be more personal, less formally established, and hence less stable than the chief's. Again, an inequality of prestige and participation is built on a system of redistribution which periodically levels the distribution of economic resources.

I have concentrated here on the levelling tendencies in the stateless primitive societies, including the redistributive systems. The *potential* for abuse of the scheme of reciprocities in the latter by big men or chiefs should be apparent. Normally, the chief who fails in his obligation to be generous with what he has received is not tolerated. But in certain circumstances (as we shall see in the next section) he is permitted to strengthen his position and to concentrate more resources in his own and his followers' hands.

I have drawn out the way in which central features of the DMP and the practice of reciprocity and redistribution can have levelling effects, especially on the distribution of economic resources, or at any rate can serve to inhibit the growth of inequality. They are not, however, *social controls* on inequality. Indeed some of these practices themselves have to be maintained by controls, by the implicit threat of sanctions. There are in fact three principal types of control used very widely in primitive societies directly to inhibit the development of inequality. We have already encountered them in Chapter 2 as among the means whereby social order is maintained in these societies. The first can be referred to summarily as the 'pressure of public opinion', and works through a variety of practices of gossip, criticism, ridicule, praise and so forth, which employ the negative sanctions of shame, of a sense of guilt and of damage to a person's public reputation, and the correlative positive sanctions of being publicly respected and esteemed. The second form of control is based on the tacit threat of withdrawal of the advantages of the system of generalised reciprocity, and in extreme cases expulsion from the community. The sanctions associated with the third form of control are accusations of witchcraft and sorcery. These three are the only practices widely used in stateless and partially stateless societies to inhibit or arrest the development of inequality which it would be proper to describe as social controls. The first and second of them are universally important, not only in primitive societies but also (as we shall see) in certain peasant and intentional communities. Witchcraft and sorcery accusations are used widely, though not universally in primitive and peasant communities, but they are of intermittent influence, a means of control of 'second resort'.

All three forms of control are used not only to maintain some of the egalitarian practices which we have already discussed (the practice of biasing generalised reciprocity in favour of those in need, for example), but also to inhibit individuals from seeking eminence or to dissuade them from maintaining it. The !Kung San call lack of generosity 'far-heartedness' and 'browbeat each other constantly to be more generous and not to hoard', just as they make derisive jokes about anyone who is at all arrogant or boastful or is successful in the hunt, 'to cool his heart and make him gentle'.[16] In the Melanesian society studied by Michael Young 'sorcery was, and still is, greatly feared by those who would display an uncommon talent or a conspicuous degree of wealth, whether this be counted in gardens, pigs, shell valuables or cash'.[17] Similarly, among the Bemba, according to Audrey Richards, 'A man who is full when others are hungry is hardly considered to have achieved the good fortune by natural means. An occasional stroke of good luck is not resented, but to be permanently more prosperous than the rest of the village would almost certainly lead to accusations of sorcery.'[18]

I turn now to a brief account of levelling mechanisms and social controls on inequality in peasant societies. It is in those peasant communities most closely resembling true communities – the closed corporate communities which I described in Section 1.5 – that we find levelling mechanisms most developed and

[16] Lee, *The !Kung San*, pp. 458, 246. [17] Young, *Fighting With Food*, p. 10.
[18] Richards, *Land, Labour and Diet in Northern Rhodesia*.

effective and indeed a greater degree of economic inequality. Nevertheless, even in these closed corporate communities there is considerable inequality.

A standard example of the closed corporate form is the peasant commune (*mir* or *obschina*) of pre-revolutionary Great Russia and Siberia. The *mir* enjoyed a considerable degree of self-government and carried out many of the functions of a local authority: it had a collective duty to ensure payment of state taxes; it was responsible for internal law enforcement and dispute settlement, for the welfare of the aged and handicapped, and for such things as road and bridge maintenance and the provision of educational facilities; its gathering could fix the dues to fund these activities. However, this communal gathering consisted only of the heads of peasant households, the non-peasant families and those without land having no representation. Further, as Shanin says, in practice decision-making in the communal gathering 'was far removed from the formally democratic proceedings laid down by law', for although 'the decisions were typically unanimous . . . the actual power lay in the hands of several of the more active and, on the whole, more wealthy, members of the community who took the lead'.[19] Notwithstanding the inequality in land holdings (in part the result of the purchasing of private land by peasant households from outside) and in participation, efforts were made to constrain the growth of inequality. The most notable levelling arrangement was the periodic repartition of land. The commune held legal title to most of the land, which it allotted to households for their use, and it had the right to redistribute this land from time to time on the basis of some more-or-less egalitarian principle.[20] According to Shanin, land redistribution

[19] Teodor Shanin, *The Awkward Class* (Oxford: Clarendon Press, 1972), p. 34.
[20] Shanin, *The Awkward Class*, pp. 36–7. See also Jerome Blum, *Lord and Peasant in Russia from the Ninth to the Nineteenth Century* (Princeton, NJ: Princeton University Press, 1961), ch. 24.

accounted for only a part of the levelling which actually occurred; also (or more) important were the 'substantive changes' in holdings caused by partitioning (for example, as junior members of the household matured and set up by themselves), merger, extinction and migration of households.[21] The egalitarianism of the *mir* is shown also in the behaviour of the peasant courts where 'the satisfaction of the minimum needs of every family and the maintenance of good neighbourhood relations were valued more highly than impartiality . . . which could account for the typical tendency of the peasant court . . . to resolve by division of property rather than to pass judgement totally in favour of one side'.[22]

The periodic redistribution of land (especially of meadowland) was not confined to Russia. It was practised in many parts of Europe, both eastern and western, where there was collective ownership of part of the land by the village community, from the Middle Ages down to the nineteenth century.[23] Nevertheless, even where land redistribution was practised, the European village was far from equal – in economic resources, in power, or in participation in the community's collective decision-making.[24]

The closed corporate peasant community is also the predominant form in Central America and the Andes. 'Levelling mechanisms are ubiquitous devices in peasant economies in this area', says Manning Nash, and he goes on to specify the levelling mechanisms found in a peasant Indian community in the Mexican state of Chiapas:[25] in addition to a certain amount of generalised reciprocity, including festive labour,[26] communal

---

[21] Shanin, *The Awkward Class*, especially ch. 5.

[22] Shanin, *The Awkward Class*, p. 41.

[23] Jerome Blum, 'The European village as community: origins and functions'.

[24] Jerome Blum, 'The internal structure and polity of the European village community', especially at pp. 549–50 and 570–4.

[25] Manning Nash, 'The social context of economic choice in a small society', *Man*, 61 (1961), 186–91.

control of some of the land, and the constraints on accumulation imposed by a simple technology and by a limited amount of land available to the community, there are two important arrangements which we have not yet encountered. The first is the practice of rotating among those most able to afford them the burdens of provisioning and financing religious ceremonies and of holding certain civil and religious offices, the costs of which can be exorbitant. The second is the practice of partible inheritance which, by dividing resources, especially land, between offspring, periodically breaks down accumulated holdings. Behind these levelling practices are the three kinds of sanctions referred to earlier: gossip, ridicule, shaming and so on; withdrawal of reciprocity; and witchcraft and sorcery. Nash writes of the 'pervasive system of belief in witchcraft' in the community he studied in Mexico: 'Witchcraft befalls those who violate the norms of familial and household harmony, who do not get along with neighbors, who are rich but not generous, who refuse communal obligations, who become outstanding in some dimension which violates the corporate nature of the community or upsets its tendency to economic homogeneity.'[27] Oscar Lewis tells us in his well-known study of *Life in a Mexican Village* that 'Gossip is unrelenting and harsh in Tepoztlán', that 'successful persons are popular targets of criticism, envy, and malicious gossip', and finally that 'Fear of sorcery is not omnipresent. It occurs only when a person has reason to expect it as a result of having injured or insulted another or of having become wealthy or otherwise outstanding.'[28] Although the

[26] For a detailed account of peasant forms of reciprocity and their bearing on inequality, see Benjamin Orlove, 'Inequality among peasants: the forms and uses of reciprocal exchange in Andean Peru', in R. Halperin and J. Dow, eds., *Peasant Livelihood: Studies in Economic Anthropology and Cultural Ecology* (New York: St Martin's Press, 1977).

[27] Nash, 'The social context of economic choice'.

[28] Oscar Lewis, *Life in a Mexican Village: Tepoztlán Restudied* (Urbana, Ill.: University of Illinois Press, 1951), p. 294.

levelling practices typical of Mesoamerican peasant communities operate in Tepoztlán and were backed by the usual social controls, so that there were not enormous disparities of wealth between households, and although equal inheritance by all children made it difficult for a family to maintain an economically superior position for very long, nevertheless at the time of Lewis's study there was considerable variation in wealth, including land holdings. It is interesting (from our point of view), though scarcely surprising, that these differences contributed, in Lewis's view, to the pervasive distrust, absence of friendship and repressed hostility between families[29] – in other words, such inequality as existed was inimical to community.

For a final illustration I turn to James Scott's account of *The Moral Economy of the Peasant* in south-east Asia. Here – and in many other peasant societies around the world – peasant standards of justice and equity and of what constitutes exploitation are based on two moral principles: the norm of reciprocity and the right to subsistence. The second principle is strongest in 'areas where the village is most autonomous and cohesive ' and is upheld by practices and social controls of the kinds we have already encountered. 'Few village studies of south-east Asia fail to remark on the informal social controls which act to provide for the minimal needs of the poor.'[30] The wealthy are expected to assist their poorer kin or neighbours, to take on more dependents and to finance and provision religious celebrations. Failing to be generous, the wealthy meet with contempt and malicious gossip (whereas generosity earns them prestige and an indebted clientele). In some communities, communal land is used to help the poor: some of it is allotted to

---

[29] Contemporary inequality was only one cause. Lewis notes (p. 292) that this was also rooted in a 'long history of conquest, colonial status and internal and external political and economic exploitation'.

[30] James C. Scott, *The Moral Economy of the Peasant: Rebellion and Subsistence in Southeast Asia* (New Haven, Conn.: Yale University Press, 1976), p. 41.

them for their use and rent from it is used in part to support them.

In the more 'open' peasant communities, which have more permeable boundaries and far more ties to the outside world (including significant cash crop production for the market, with outside capitalisation), land is privately owned and the community has no control over the individual's disposition of it. All three forms of social control discussed above are found in these communities but they are not used to inhibit ostentatious consumption or the development of inequality as they are in the closed corporate community. The open community is therefore much more unequal economically. It is also less of a true community than the closed corporate community: relations between households are less frequently direct and many-sided and there is less reciprocity between them, some of it being displaced by cooperation and exchange with outsiders.[31]

We have seen that the social controls which are used in primitive and peasant societies to contain inequality are among those used for the maintenance of social order which were described in Chapter 2. That similar sorts of controls are used in both contexts is, I think, in large part a consequence of the limited range of means of control available to stateless and semi-stateless societies. Even if it were the case that an increase in equality or the containment of inequality is a non-excludable public good (as is the maintenance of social order, with the qualifications noted in Chapter 2), there is no necessary reason why the means of ensuring its provision should be the same; and in fact some of the means by which order is maintained in stateless societies do not play a part in inhibiting the growth of inequality. But is there in fact a non-excludable public good, and hence also a potential free rider problem, involved in redistribution?

[31] Eric R. Wolf, 'Types of Latin American peasantry'.

For a redistribution of resources in the direction of greater equality to be a public good it must in the first place be a move which is preferred by every member of the public. There are two principal grounds for such a preference. It may result not from a desire for increased equality *per se* but from a combination of risk-aversion and uncertainty about one's economic future. Such a preference (for a system which taxed those presently better off to give to those in need) could be said to embody 'altruism towards one's later selves', but it would be more plainly described as an egoistic preference for (self-)insurance. Alternatively, a person might prefer redistribution if he is sufficiently altruistic, that is to say, if he desires improvements in the positions of those in whose favour the distribution is to be changed. An egalitarian redistribution would clearly be a non-excludable public good for the group consisting of the altruists together with the beneficiaries, for any such redistribution benefits each of the altruists (as well as the beneficiaries) whether or not he contributed to it in any way. There is thus *potentially* a free rider problem: an individual may desire redistribution but would prefer it to be financed or provisioned out of others' holdings, leaving his own intact. If richer individuals prefer poorer ones to have more income than they could otherwise secure by their own efforts, then income redistribution could in this way be justified by appeal to the Pareto criterion,[32] and if there is a free rider problem, then for those who accept the liberal theory of the state discussed (and rejected) in Chapter 2, progressive taxation raised coercively by the state is also justified. A similar argument can be used to justify a National Health Service – or at any rate arrangements

[32] H. H. Hochman and J. D. Rodgers, 'Pareto optimal redistribution', *American Economic Review*, 59 (1969), 542–57. See also Lester C. Thurow, 'The income distribution as a public good', *Quarterly Journal of Economics*, 85 (1971), 327–33, and James D. Rodgers, 'Explaining income redistribution', in H. H. Hochman and G. E. Peterson, eds., *Redistribution Through Public Choice* (New York: Columbia University Press, 1974).

which make medical aid available to all and are financed out of compulsory progressive taxation – just as long as it is reasonable to assume that the better off are concerned for the health of the poorer.[33]

I have said only that there is *potentially* a free rider problem here. It is easily shown that if one of the altruists is *sufficiently* altruistic, it is rational for him to contribute *something* whether others do or not. In general, even in this one-shot redistribution and even leaving aside complications due to strategic interaction between individuals, the optimal amount of an individual's contribution depends on his utility function (taking account of the degree of his altruism) and on the transformation function.[34]

The altruistic preference of the rich for redistribution may of course be the product of an 'enlightened' egoism – a calculation, for example, that sharing some of their wealth with the poor is necessary to avert revolt, to keep production going and so to maintain their position, or that contributing to the health of the poor will enhance the healthiness of their own environment or improve their profits. But whatever its motive, it is very unlikely that the required altruism would be sufficiently widespread among the rich to make a redistributive system a public good for the whole society.[35]

A preference for a redistributive 'welfare' system based on the insurance model is likely to be more widespread in any society. In a society in which power and economic position are very unequally distributed, there is unlikely to be a unanimous preference for any particular system and indeed there may be some individuals, confident of their economic future, who

[33] This argument has been made by A. J. Culyer, *Need and the National Health Service* (London: Martin Robertson, 1976). See also A. J. Culyer, *The Political Economy of Social Policy* (Oxford: Martin Robertson, 1980) and Kenneth J. Arrow, 'Uncertainty and the economics of medical care', *American Economic Review*, 53 (1963), 941–73.

[34] See Taylor, *Anarchy and Cooperation*, ch. 2.

[35] See Rodgers, 'Explaining income redistribution'.

would not want to participate in any such system.[36] But in the much more egalitarian stateless and quasi-stateless communities which we have been looking at, *nobody* can be confident that he will not one day find himself among the needy, so that every individual, facing an uncertain future and taking a very dim view of the prospect of household failure, has a preference for redistributive arrangements based on the insurance motive. But he would of course prefer *others* to maintain these arrangements, to benefit from them when he is in need but not to contribute when he is able to. It is possible that levelling arrangements (including generalised reciprocity biased in favour of those in need) could be maintained as a result of all the participants adopting strategies of conditional cooperation; but this seems unlikely, in view of the irregular and asymmetric nature of the giving and receiving. In practice, as we have seen, sanctions are used and threatened to ensure that the temporarily better off contribute to the maintenance of the system. These controls can be especially effective in this context, since at any time they need be directed against only a small number of individuals who are momentarily well off.

A free rider problem may also arise in another way which bears directly on the maintenance of equality in stateless and quasi-stateless communities. Among a group of people who try to distribute goods and services in conformity with the principle 'to each according to his needs' (regardless of work or capital contributed), an individual may be tempted to be a malingerer, to work less than he is able or less than is expected of him. The problem arises in those intentional communities – such as the nineteenth- and twentieth-century utopian communities and the *kibbutzim* and *shitufim* of Israel – where there is approximately equal access to communal property and equal availability of

---

[36] See Rodgers, 'Explaining income redistribution'.

collectively produced goods and services (in some cases subject to everyone's needs first being satisfied), regardless of labour and capital contributed.[37] More generally, any group which distributes to its members benefits which are independent of their contributions (or largely so) is liable to be taken advantage of by free riders. Such a system of distribution constitutes a public good: it is indivisible, though in practice not perfectly so. It is also, by definition, non-excludable, since anyone may benefit from the provision of goods or services even though he or she has not contributed.

The American and British utopian communities of the nineteenth and twentieth centuries and the Israeli *kibbutzim* and *shitufim* are quasi-anarchic, in the sense indicated in Section 1.5. Most of these were egalitarian so far as benefits were concerned, but nearly all of them were troubled by an inequality of work effort. In the great majority of the nineteenth-century American communities studied by R. M. Kanter, the community owned everything of importance (from land and buildings to furniture, tools, equipment and even clothing and personal effects); individuals signed over their property on admission to the community, either irreversibly or for the duration of their membership; community services were freely available to all and accommodation, food, clothing and other goods were distributed for consumption or use either equally or on the basis of need; there was no compensation for labour; and in about half of the communities jobs were rotated. *All* of these

---

[37] 'To each according to his needs' is of course not necessarily an egalitarian principle. It might and typically does require that people be treated unequally. As it stands it is incomplete, since it does not specify the distribution of any surplus which may be left over when everyone's needs are satisfied. However, it can be – and where it is practised it usually is – interpreted in an egalitarian spirit (the point of treating people differently so as to satisfy their different needs being to bring them up to a roughly equal level of well-being) and where the needs of all can be satisfied its natural extension (as David Miller has argued) is to divide the surplus equally. Miller, *Social Justice* (Oxford: Clarendon Press, 1976), ch.4.

practices were found more frequently in what Kanter calls the 'successful' communities (those which lasted as utopian communities for at least twenty-five years) than in the unsuccessful ones.[38] There were exceptions to this pattern of course; chief among them were the nineteen Owenite communities of the 1820s and the thirty-odd Fourierist communities of the 1840s, nearly all of them short-lived: these were less egalitarian, payment being made according to work or capital contributed; but then they were rather weak as communities, for their members were a heterogeneous lot, generally lacking shared interests and goals.[39]

Communal ownership, egalitarian payment (with needs taken into account) regardless of contribution, freely available services and approximately equal consumption of goods also characterise the Israeli *kibbutzim* and *shitufim*. The wave of communes founded in America and Britain in the 1960s and 1970s cannot be lumped straightforwardly with the nineteenth-century communities or with these Israeli communities. Although the ideology in nearly all of them is egalitarian, in very many – probably most of them – the practice is a little different. But although the land, the buildings and most of their contents are not collectively owned and there are often considerable differences in wealth and income brought into the commune and wealth and income are very rarely shared, nevertheless there is usually a shared (and roughly equal) use of the land, buildings, facilities, equipment and some personal effects, while household chores are rotated and consumption does not vary widely.

In virtually all of these communities, of all three kinds,

---

[38] Rosabeth Moss Kanter, *Commitment and Community: Communes and Utopias in Sociological Perspective* (Cambridge, Mass.: Harvard University Press, 1972), pp. 104–5.

[39] See Charles J. Erasmus, *In Search of the Common Good: Utopian Experiments Past and Future* (New York: Free Press, 1977), pp. 144–6, and Kanter, *Commitment and Community*, pp. 93–4 and 122–3.

efforts are made to maintain an approximate equality of status, and where leaders and authorities and people of outstanding drive or ability do arise the community is likely to go out of its way to see that no special privileges or material advantages are granted to them. The important exception to this is that many (though probably a minority) of the nineteenth-century communes and a few of the twentieth-century communes were founded by a charismatic leader, who had very great authority (though still in the sense described in Section 1.3) and in some cases special privileges, including finer housing than the rest of the community.[40]

In all these intentional communities *a central problem was inequality of work effort*. Every adult member of a community was expected to put in a certain number of hours of work, or to contribute as much labour as he was able; but since an individual's rewards were not dependent on the amount or quality of his work, there was always the temptation to be a free rider on the efforts of others – to find excuses for not working some days, to put little effort into the work, to contribute the minimum amount of work acceptable. There are few studies of any of these communities which do not furnish examples of such free riders, and it is my impression that it is the chief source of discontent in contemporary communes.[41]

How did these communities attempt to deter free riders? The full withdrawal of reciprocity was not practised (if it had been, the system of distribution would no longer have been a non-excludable public good), but ostracism and various degrees of exclusion from the social life of the community were practised and permanent ejection from the community was an extreme sanction occasionally used. I have not been able to discover any

---

[40] See Kanter, *Commitment and Community*, ch. 4, and Erasmus, *In Search of the Common Good*, ch. 5.
[41] For some examples from nineteenth-century American communes see Erasmus, *In Search of the Common Good*, pp. 144–5 and 160–2.

examples of the use of witchcraft or sorcery accusations in these communities – although in the religious communities the spiritual leaders could often make use of implicit threats of supernatural sanctions. The principal controls which were explicitly brought to bear on these free riders were those based on shame, public approval and disapproval, denunciation, criticism and ridicule. In very many of the nineteenth-century utopian communities and in the *kibbutzim* and *shitufim* (but not in many contemporary communes) these methods were institutionalised. Charles Nordhoff describes 'the institution of Criticism' used by the Perfectionists of Oneida 'as their main instrument of government'.[42] Members were expected to volunteer to submit themselves from time to time to criticism by the whole assembled community or by a committee of those best acquainted with them. This was in addition to 'daily evening meetings, which all are expected to attend' and in which 'religious, social, and business matters are freely discussed, and opportunity given for exhortation and reproof'.[43] Mutual confession was practised at Amana, but only at annual meetings, and the Rappites at Harmony conducted weekly 'mutual improvement' meetings.[44] Again, the successful (long-lived) communities in Kanter's nineteenth-century sample were more likely to have institutionalised these methods of public criticism, denunciation, and so on, than were the unsuccessful communities.[45]

Similar methods of control of free riders are used in the *kibbutzim* and *shitufim* (though not in the dramatic forms sometimes found in the nineteenth-century communes). Public

---

[42] Charles Nordhoff, *The Communistic Societies of the United States* (New York: Schocken, 1965), p. 289.

[43] Nordhoff, *The Communistic Societies*, p. 289, quoting John Humphrey Noyes, the founder and head of the Perfectionists.

[44] Bertha M. Shambaugh, *Amana That Was and Amana That Is* (Iowa City: State Historical Society of Iowa, 1932), p. 247; Aaron Williams, *The Harmony Society at Economy, Pennsylvania* (Pittsburgh: W. S. Haven, 1866), p. 41.

criticism by the entire assembly is a potent sanction, and the threat of it is usually effective in dealing with malingerers, when grillings by various supervisors and by a management committee have failed. The ultimate sanction, seldom employed, was expulsion from the community (on a vote of the assembly).[46] As we would expect, these informal controls do not operate as effectively in the *moshavim*, which are less communal than the *kibbutzim* and where people do fewer things together and generally spend less time in direct contact with each other.[47]

It is interesting to compare the experience of the cases so far considered with the well-known Chinese and Cuban attempts (and less radical or less persistent attempts in other 'communist' countries) to narrow the range of incomes and equalise access to public services, while motivating workers with 'non-material' or 'moral' incentives. During the 1960s, especially during the 'Revolutionary Offensive' of 1966–70, the Cuban government greatly increased the provision of free public services, including education, public transport, medical care, and water, gas and electricity. At the same time, there were very few consumer goods, apart from food, available to spend wages on, most were rationed and prices were fixed at low levels. With employment, a minimum wage and housing guaranteed as well, there was clearly potential for free riding, and indeed absenteeism and general malingering became widespread. Combined with these egalitarian policies in this period was an effort by the government to replace material rewards in part by non-material incentives. These all made use of the positive sanctions of public approval

[45] Kanter, *Commitment and Community*, p. 112.
[46] Melford Spiro, *Kibbutz: Venture in Utopia* (New York: Schocken, 1963), pp. 90–109.
[47] Richard D. Schwartz, 'Social control in two Israeli settlements', in D. Black and M. Mileski, eds., *The Social Organization of Law* (New York: Seminar Press, 1973).

and disapproval. Good workers were praised in bulletins and on factory notice boards by political leaders and managers and were awarded certificates, plaques and so on, while less productive workers were publicly criticised and shamed. The Cuban economy seems to have become less productive as a result of this campaign and during the 1970s the government increased the use of material incentives and the differentials between them.[48]

In China, similar methods were used, especially during the Great Leap Forward period of 1958–60, apparently with similar results and again leading to a revival of material rewards. Apart from this period and that of the Great Proletarian Cultural Revolution of 1966–9, Chinese agriculture has become more productive since the Revolution. Two of the important reasons for this are of interest here. First, the groups within which work is organised are small: brigades are divided into work teams of 20–30 households which in turn are usually divided into work groups of only 4–10 households. Second, much of the Chinese population has been organised into *hsiao tsu*, small groups of 8–15 individuals, which are used by the government for exerting pressure on the masses. These groups, organised in factories, urban neighbourhoods and government offices, in military units and peasant work teams, meet regularly for political study and their members engage in mutual- and self-criticism. They are instruments of social control in general and are used in particular to move people to work harder. China observers agree that the *hsiao tsu* have been effective, and undoubtedly this has been made possible by the adoption of the small group setting. But their effectiveness has been limited because, despite their small size, these groups are far from being little communities: they are not made up of close neighbours,

[48] See Robert M. Bernardo, *The Theory of Moral Incentives in Cuba* (University, Alabama: The University of Alabama Press, 1971), and Archibald Ritter, *The Economic Development of Revolutionary Cuba* (New York: Praeger, 1974).

friends or kin (indeed are intentionally formed by the cadres so as to cut across the naturally occurring groups, whose pressures and socialising influence they are in part designed to counteract).[49]

If the attempts made in both Cuba and China to deal with the free rider problems involved in meeting individuals' basic material needs, regardless of their contribution, and increasing the availability of free public services (both of which, together with the narrowing of the range of wages, helped to diminish economic inequality) were not entirely successful, one of the reasons, I submit, is that these large-scale state-directed campaigns were not based on small communities. That the Chinese attempt has been more successful than the Cuban is due in part to the fact that they simulated and took advantage of *some* of the features of the small community.

In an interesting recent contribution Joseph Carens has argued that moral incentives *can* be relied on to motivate people to put forth work effort in a society in which one kind of economic equality, namely equality of after-tax incomes, is assured.[50] In his 'essay in utopian politico-economic theory' he considers a rational-choice model of an egalitarian system which is just like a private property market (or PPM) system save that annual after-tax incomes for consumption are distributed equally among adult individuals. Of the logically necessary prerequisites for the egalitarian system to function as effectively

[49] Charles Hoffman, *Work Incentive Practices and Policies in the People's Republic of China 1953–1965* (Albany, NY: State University of New York Press, 1967); Charles Hoffman, *The Chinese Worker* (Albany, NY: State University of New York Press, 1974); Christopher Howe, 'Labour organization and incentives in industry, before and after the Cultural Revolution', in Stuart Schram, ed., *Authority, Participation, and Cultural Change in China* (Cambridge: Cambridge University Press, 1973); Martin King Whyte, *Small Groups and Political Rituals in China* (Berkeley: University of California Press, 1974); R. J. Birrell, 'The centralized control of the communes in the post-"Great Leap" period', in A. Doak Barnett, ed., *Chinese Communist Politics in Action* (Seattle: University of Washington Press, 1969).

[50] Joseph A. Carens, *Equality, Moral Incentives, and the Market: An Essay in Utopian Politico-Economic Theory* (Chicago: University of Chicago Press, 1981).

as the PPM system, the crucial ones are that individuals believe they have a social duty to earn as much pre-tax income as they are capable of earning, that they derive satisfaction from performing this social duty and that they place the same relative value on these social-duty satisfactions as individuals in the PPM system place on the income-consumption satisfactions. If individuals are equipped with the moral incentives contained in these three prerequisites (and assuming that the other logical prerequisites are met), it can be shown that the egalitarian system will function as efficiently as the PPM system and in particular that it will not suffer from work-shyness on the part of its members.

The question now obviously arises, how might individuals come to have preferences of the kind required by these logical prerequisites of the egalitarian system, or, what *empirical* conditions must be met if the logical prerequisites are to be realised in the real world? In his answer to this question, Carens relies almost exclusively on socialisation. 'There must be an effective socialisation process which causes people in the egalitarian system to value the social approval and self-esteem gained from performing one's social duty.' Furthermore, there must be widespread commitment to the norm of equal income distribution and this too 'would have to be created through socialization to the norm of income equality'.[51] While Carens recognises that the socialisation process in the egalitarian system would have to be more intense than the corresponding socialisation which leads people in the PPM system to value income-consumption satisfactions, nevertheless, it seems to me that his reliance on socialisation alone is indeed 'utopian' in the light of the evidence from the egalitarian anarchic communities considered here. I am not thinking of the Chinese and Cuban experiences, which were, amongst other things, too

---

[51] Carens, *Equality, Moral Incentives, and the Market*, pp. 175–6.

short-lived to be conclusive, but of the primitive anarchies and peasant quasi-anarchies where, despite intense socialisation aimed at producing people who value 'social approval and self-esteem', there is nevertheless a need for social controls to contain the growth of economic inequality.

I argued in Section 2.5 that the two most important social controls used to maintain order in stateless societies – those based on reciprocity and on approval and disapproval – together depend on community for their effectiveness. The same pair of social controls are the central means of containing the growth of inequality in stateless and quasi-stateless societies, and require the same conditions to be effective.

These controls are themselves egalitarian, in the sense that there is wide participation in their operation. Indeed, since they occupy such an important place in *anarchies*, they *must* be egalitarian; for, as I remarked in Section 1.2, to the extent that a society lacks political specialisation and concentration of force, there must be equal participation in whatever political functions remain, and these always include the redistribution of resources as well as the maintenance of internal and external security and making collective decisions. Wide participation in politics itself tends to inhibit the growth of economic inequality. But this would not suffice alone. It must be supplemented by some sort of controls, and in the absence of the state these controls are made effective by community. A rough equality, then, *can* survive in an anarchy, provided that the anarchy is also a community.

3.3 The birth of the state

The argument of Chapter 2 is that 'anarchy requires community'. The argument of the last section is that 'community requires a rough equality and the maintenance of this equality in anarchy requires community'. Community is what makes egalitarian anarchy possible. But it does not suffice to guarantee its survival. The closest historical (or prehistorical) approximations to the pure egalitarian anarchic community are the primitive societies which I have referred to as acephalous. In such societies *Homo sapiens* lived for nearly all of his forty or fifty thousand years, just as all the other hominids had done for several million years. But now these anarchic communities have almost everywhere disappeared – absorbed, undermined or destroyed by states. A detailed account of how and why this happened, and especially how the very first states arose independently of other states, would carry me too far from the main lines of my argument, but a brief sketch is in order for the light it throws on the relations between community, anarchy and equality and on the stability of the egalitarian anarchic community and future prospects for a durable anarchy.

The formation of states in most societies has been the direct or indirect result, at least in part, of the presence nearby of already existing states. These *secondary* formations of states are relatively easy to understand. Societies without a state are subjugated, colonised or absorbed by states. Or, feeling threatened or actually attacked by a neighbouring state, a stateless society becomes more militarily organised, and previously existing leaders and authorities are granted the control of concentrated force, then go on to emulate the model of government they have before them in the states which threaten them. Or an expanding neighbouring state encroaches on their land or other resources and sets in train internal processes (to be described below) which lead to state formation. So the egalitarian anarchic community, though it can last for millennia if left alone, is terribly vulnerable to other states.

More difficult to account for is the *primary* or *pristine* development of a state, without the influence or model of an already formed state.[52] The only instances of primary state formation are generally thought to be those which occurred in Mesopotamia, Egypt, the Indus River Valley, North China, Mesoamerica and Peru – though there is controversy about the degrees to which the last five of these six cases were affected by earlier and contemporary political developments in other areas in this group (it being agreed that state formation in Mesopotamia, during the fourth and third millennia BC, takes temporal priority).[53] How did these primary states arise?

One account which is of special interest here (although I shall reject it) is the 'Marxist' account.[54] Briefly, the argument is that technological advance (and in particular the development of agriculture) makes possible for the first time and in fact automatically brings into existence a food surplus, which leads to trade and the production of commodities for exchange; thus entrepreneurs, merchants, various kinds of craftsmen and other specialists arise (freed by the existence of a food surplus from participating in food production); out of this division of labour and exchange activity develops economic inequality, leading eventually to stratification into social classes based on differential access to important means of production; and finally the state is formed by the class with privileged access to the means of production in order to maintain this system of stratification.

It should be said that many of the writers who subscribe to the more characteristically Marxist part of the theory (stratifi-

---

[52] The distinction between 'pristine' and 'secondary' formations is due to Morton H. Fried, *The Evolution of Political Society*.

[53] There are brief accounts of all six of these primary formations in Elman R. Service, *Origins of the State and Civilization* (New York: Norton, 1975).

[54] See especially Frederick Engels, *The Origin of the Family, Private Property and the State* (London: Lawrence and Wishart, 1972); Lewis Henry Morgan, *Ancient Society* (Cambridge, Mass.: Harvard University Press, 1964), which was Engels' principal source; and V. Gordon Childe, *Man Makes Himself* (London: Watts, 1936). Recent variants include Lawrence Krader, *Formation of the State* (Englewood Cliffs, NJ: Prentice-Hall, 1968); Fried, *The Evolution of Political Society*; and several of the contributions to Henri J. M. Claessen and Peter Skalnik, eds., *The Early State* (The Hague: Mouton, 1978).

cation leading to state formation) do *not* subscribe to the first step in the argument, namely that technological advance, and in particular the development of agriculture, automatically creates a food surplus. Primitive agriculturalists produce only to meet their needs (and the most primitive agriculturalists, like hunters and gatherers, could do this in only two to four hours of 'work' per day), and in the absence of any pressures they appear never to want to intensify their efforts.[55] Sahlins writes of the Domestic Mode of Production (which I described in the last section) that it is 'intrinsically an anti-surplus system', and he goes on to show how the intensification of production so as to produce a surplus is stimulated *by central political leadership*.[56] In the case of chiefdoms this stimulation is prompted by the chief's desire to be ever more liberal and so build and maintain a following. With increasing political specialisation and concentration of force, the need for the production of surpluses is obvious.[57]

The summary given above of the 'Marxist' theory of the origin of the state glosses over differences between variants, but common to all versions is the idea that a considerable degree of economic inequality is causally prior to state formation. The evidence does not give this proposition a great deal of support. Much of the evidence which has been offered in support of it shows only that the primary states, not long after their emergence, were economically stratified. But this is of course consistent also with the simultaneous rise, *pari passu*, of political and economic stratification, or with the *prior* development of the state – i.e. of *political* stratification – and the creation of economic stratification by the ruling class. This last alternative is argued most explicitly by Elman Service in his

[55] Marshall Sahlins, *Stone Age Economics*, chs. 1 and 2.
[56] *Stone Age Economics*, ch. 3.
[57] See Karl Polanyi, Conrad M. Arensberg and Harry W. Pearson, eds., *Trade and Market in the Early Empires* (Glencoe, Ill.: Free Press, 1957), especially Part III, for some interesting discussions of this theme.

recent survey of *The Origins of the State and Civilization*. 'In all of the archaic civilizations and historically known chiefdoms and primitive states', he writes, 'the "stratification" was . . . mainly of two classes, the governors and the governed – political strata, not strata of ownership groups.' And he goes on to argue that in none of these cases does a governing stratum use force to maintain its position. 'At least this is not recorded in the historical cases, nor is it visible in the archaeological record. In other words, there apparently was no class conflict resulting in forceful repression.'[58]

I have singled out for rejection the 'Marxist' account of the origin of the state because of its bearing on the relation between community and equality and also because, of the several early theories,[59] this is the only one which still has some (though diminishing) support. Community requires a measure of economic equality and, as I argued in the last section, the maintenance of approximate economic equality in the absence of a state requires community. In the Marxist account it is the development of gross economic inequality which gives rise to state formation (and in the process weakens communities). But in more recent accounts, including the hybrid which emerges from the following discussion (and which seems least inconsistent with the evidence as well as telling a plausible story), the weakening of community and the development of gross inequality are the *concomitants* and *consequences* of state formation.

Having rejected the 'class conflict' account of the rise of the state, Service himself goes on to offer an explanation which lays great stress on the *integrative* role of the emerging central power, on its voluntary acceptance by the people in virtue of its

---

[58] Service, *Origins of the State and Civilization*, p. 285.
[59] For critical summaries of the main ones, see Service, *Origins of the State and Civilization*, chs. 2 and 16; Ronald Cohen, 'State origins: a reappraisal', ch. 2 in Claessen and Skalnik, eds., *The Early State*; and Kent V. Flannery, 'The cultural evolution of civilizations', *Annual Review of Ecology and Systematics*, 3 (1972), 399–426.

work in the common interest.[60] The germ of state formation lies in the leaders who are universally found in acephalous societies. They are no more than authorities (in the sense described in Section 1.3) but their advice and direction is sought and heeded in particular circumstances. In some of these societies, where circumstances are favourable, centralised redistribution develops. The conditions which most favour the growth of centralised redistribution exist in regions having a number of different ecological niches. If these are settled (possibly as a result of fission), they will be exploited in partially differing ways and the exchange of local specialities may be mutually advantageous. The resulting system of exchanges may favour one village (perhaps because of its central location, or because it is the parent community, the others having split off from it), and if the village has a man with a following, his position is much enhanced, as he becomes the centre of the system of redistribution for all the exchanging communities. If he does this job well and there are benefits all round, his prestige rises accordingly. The chief's prestige will also be enhanced in the measure that he successfully acquits himself in his other valued roles – in arbitrating disputes, for example, and carrying out public works and coordinating defence against external threats. The chief, then, is given the support of his people because he provides them with benefits. But this does not explain how the central leadership comes to have power based on concentrated force, which is the hallmark of the state.

At this point, Service suggests[61] that 'the coherence of the collectivity' (and by implication, I think, the position of the central leadership too) is strengthened by a 'threatening environment', and two things above all tend to make an environment threatening: first, the territory of the society in question

---

[60] Service, *Origins of the State and Civilization*, chs. 4 and 17.
[61] *Origins of the State and Civilization*, p. 298.

is circumscribed by such natural features as mountains, deserts and seas, so that expansion and flight are impossible; second, there are enemy or rival societies nearby. For Service, the point about these two constraints is that they make membership in a polity with an already beneficial, legitimate leadership even more attractive. What he does not add is that they tend to lead to an increase in the use of force or at least an accumulation of the means of using force (for obvious reasons in the case of defence; for reasons I'll return to shortly in the case of geographic circumscription). It would then be plausible to argue (in the spirit of Service's general approach) that the 'threatening environment' *also* tends to make a concentration of the means of using force and of actual force acceptable, especially if they are concentrated (as they are in practice, of course) in the hands of the already existing central redistributive leadership.

To understand properly this last part of the argument, we need to go back to what, in my view, should be the starting point of any account of the origins of states, namely the process of *fissioning*, which Service has little to say about. For it is the tendency to fission which has to be overcome if a state is to be formed.[62] Fissioning is a normal part of the life of all stateless societies – in chiefdoms and big-man systems as well as in strictly acephalous societies. When a local community in such a society grows too large for its members to work local land, a part of it splits off and establishes a replicate community on new land. The same thing happens in cases of persistent internal conflict, the disaffected or unpopular faction moving

---

[62] Ronald Cohen, who has emphasised fissioning more than any other writer on state formation, has even proposed that its absence should be used as the key diagnostic for the presence of a state. See 'The political system', in R. Naroll and R. Cohen, eds., *A Handbook of Method in Cultural Anthropology* (New York: Natural History Press, 1971), and his Introduction to R. Cohen and E. R. Service, eds., *Origins of the State: The Anthropology of Political Evolution* (Philadelphia: Institute for the Study of Human Issues, 1978).

out to establish an autonomous community elsewhere. This, as I noted earlier (in Section 2.5), facilitates the maintenance of social order without a state, by removing sources of disorder and by keeping the community small enough for it to remain a true community, hence able to operate effectively the alternative social controls. If, instead of fissioning, the community continues to grow or is joined with others, then the resulting society eventually becomes weaker as a *community* (so that, if the argument of Chapter 2 is correct, the traditional stateless social controls become less effective and would have to be supplemented and in part displaced by social controls which depend on centralised force).

Why should the normal, age-old process of fissioning cease? The general (almost tautological) answer is that splitting off and founding a new settlement elsewhere becomes impossible or undesirable (less preferable, that is, than remaining). Proliferation of communities by fissioning is *possible*, of course, only so long as sufficiently productive land and other resources required for subsistence are available.[63] One important circumstance in which this condition is *not* met is where a society with a growing population occupies agricultural land which is narrowly circumscribed geographically. The theory of state formation developed by Robert Carneiro focuses almost exclusively on this environmental circumscription, arguing that it was the one thing which the six areas of primary state formation had in common.[64] His argument runs as follows. When normal village fissioning, caused by population growth, had filled all the available agricultural land, cultivation was intensified. Further pressure on the land led to fighting over this now scarce resource, the defeated communities being either required to pay tribute to the victors or incorporated in their political unit.

[63] Ronald Cohen, 'State origins: a reappraisal'.
[64] Robert L. Carneiro, 'A theory of the origin of the state', *Science,* 169 (1970), 733–8.

In this way, driven by population pressure on the land, progressively larger political units fought one another. The need to organise a regular flow of tribute stimulated the rise of a central administrative apparatus, and the warfare itself, being practised on an ever larger scale and more continuously, necessarily had to become more specialised (no longer involving the whole active male population part-time) and more centralised. The upshot of this process was the emergence of a state. In the numerous short and narrow valleys of coastal Peru – each of them flanked by desert and terminated by mountains and sea – 'ecological' or 'demographic' pressure, says Carneiro, led first to the formation of chiefdoms which arose from the fighting between villages, then to fighting between ever larger chiefdoms until each valley was unified under a victorious chief, the resulting valley-wide polity being sufficiently large and centralised to be deemed a state, and finally to fighting between valleys and the formation of a single empire embracing the whole of Peru.

As a complete account of the rise of the state, the circumscription theory is inadequate. While Peruvian valleys were undoubtedly circumscribed, and the Nile valley too, though less severely, it would be an exaggeration to describe in this way the areas in which primary states arose in Mesopotamia, North China and Mesoamerica (and indeed it appears at least doubtful that state formation in these areas was preceded by an increase in demographic pressure).[65] Furthermore, states did *not* arise (before European influence made itself felt) in other well-populated areas which *were* circumscribed.[66]

---

[65] See, for example, Robert McC. Adams, *The Evolution of Urban Society: Early Mesopotamia and Prehispanic Mexico* (Chicago: Aldine, 1966), ch. 2, but also T. Culyer Young, Jr, 'Population densities in early Mesopotamian urbanism', in P. J. Ucko *et al.*, eds., *Man, Settlement and Urbanism* (London: Duckworth, 1972).

[66] D. Webster, 'Warfare and the evolution of the state: a reconsideration', *American Antiquity*, 40 (1975), 464–70.

But although geographic circumscription does not suffice to explain the origins of the primary states, there is no doubt that it was *one* of the factors encouraging political integration by making fission impossible or too costly. Strict geographical circumscription would not be necessary to inhibit fission. If the agricultural land varies greatly in productive potential (as was the case in the non-strictly circumscribed primary state areas),[67] then splitting off and forming a new community would be unattractive, because relatively costly, once all the better land had been occupied. Another factor which would have made fission costly is 'circumscription' by, or even the mere proximity of, enemy or rival societies. I mentioned this earlier, together with geographical circumscription, as one aspect of a 'threatening environment' which, in Service's view, has the effect of strengthening leadership by making it more acceptable. We can add now that it also inhibits fission (thus enlarging the polity united under one leadership) by making this costly, for the presence of enemies not only prevents expansion but makes the independent community, newly formed by fission, vulnerable to attack. The presence of enemies may not merely inhibit the normal process of fissioning; actual fighting or the threat of it may prompt a fusion of communities.

The position we have arrived at, then, is that state formation has its roots not in the growth of economic inequality but in the combination of conditions which strengthen the leadership that is found in every stateless society and conditions which make fission impossible or undesirable. (Certain conditions are conducive to both of these developments, others to only one of them.) Leadership is strengthened when it provides 'service', discharging its functions to the satisfaction of the community. It is further strengthened, and may be permitted the use of a measure of concentrated force and the power which this

---

[67] Webster, 'Warfare and the evolution of the state'.

entails, when the community is put under strain, for example by ecological pressures or external enemies (or both) and, as a result, unusually great demands are made on the leadership (for example, to settle the land-use disputes which arise from more intensive agriculture).[68] Some of these latter conditions would *also* inhibit fission.

Most state formations, as I noted earlier, are secondary. They owe their development at least in part to the direct or indirect influence of already formed states. If they are not actually subjugated, colonised or absorbed by other states, the reactions of these societies to the presence of states is likely to be the same as the reactions to external threats of the societies which gave birth to the primary states.[69] That this reaction should have been so common is little to be wondered at; but insofar as any lessons for the future can be drawn from this account of how anarchic communities first gave way to (primary or secondary) states, we can say that it inspires little optimism about the viability of anarchy in a crowded world and even less optimism about the prospects for the emergence and durability of an anarchy set in a sea of states.

[68] Ronald Cohen, 'State origins: a reappraisal', and Robert McC. Netting, 'Sacred power and centralization: aspects of political adaptation in Africa', in B. Spooner, ed., *Population Growth: Anthropological Implications* (Cambridge, Mass.: MIT Press, 1972).

[69] For examples of these secondary formation processes, see Ronald Cohen, 'The natural history of hierarchy: a case study', in T. Burns and W. Buckley, eds., *Power and Control: Social Structures and their Transformation* (London and Beverly Hills: Sage, 1976), and Service, *Origins of the State and Civilization*, chs. 5–9.

4

Community and liberty

It should already be clear from the first three chapters of the book that the (small, stable) community is not a continuously harmonious place, in which necessarily there are no tensions, no social constraints on individual action, no occasions on which some individuals are persuaded, induced and even forced by others to do things they otherwise would not have done. We have seen, indeed, that community makes possible the effective use of social controls which are an alternative to the concentrated force of the state. These controls, the use of which is widely dispersed among the community's members, may be thought of as more egalitarian than those associated with the state, less liable to be used for purposes not widely approved; but they are controls nevertheless: because of them people are deterred from doing things they otherwise would do. It is not *obvious*, then, that the small community is a place in which individual liberty flourishes. Writers of a liberal persuasion have, indeed, generally claimed that community is inimical to liberty. So far as the communal societies of the pre-capitalist past are concerned, Marx largely shared this liberal assessment;[1] but he also asserted (especially in the *Grundrisse*) that, while capitalism required and established only a limited sort of liberty, it created

---

[1] In 'The British rule in India' Marx wrote that the village communities of India 'restrained the human mind within the smallest possible compass, making it the unresisting tool of superstition, enslaving it beneath traditional rules, . . . this undignified, stagnatory, and vegetative life . . . this passive sort of existence . . . these little communities [that] subjugated man to external circumstances' and so on.

the material conditions for a form of liberty not previously found, the 'free individuality' which would flourish in the communal society of the post-capitalist future.

For writers in the communitarian anarchist tradition, community is thought to be not only compatible with individual liberty but a necessary condition of it. But this relation between liberty, itself usually assumed to be the central ideal, and community is for these writers almost axiomatic or is an immediate consequence of (usually implicit) definitions of liberty. The examination of the competing claims about the compatibility of community and liberty to which this chapter is devoted is not motivated by or founded on an assumption that individual liberty (of any sort) is the central goal or even one worthwhile goal among others. My aim is to give a partial defence of community, which is at the centre of the argument of this book, against the liberal criticism, to show that, even if great value were attached to individual liberty, the small community would not stand condemned. This does not oblige me to demonstrate – what communitarian anarchists (and Marx when writing of the post-capitalist future) tend to assume – that liberty, of the appropriate kind, is maximised in, or is possible only in, community. My conclusion cannot be so strong as this.

With this as its aim, my argument obviously must not be confined to consideration of a stipulative definition of liberty which is such that the compatibility of community and liberty follows trivially, and it ought to include consideration of the accounts of liberty used in the liberal claims about the incompatibility of community and liberty. So I shall consider three notions of individual liberty. Of these, only one (which I'll call 'pure negative freedom') is strictly a concept of liberty, according to some writers. But the other two – 'freedom from coercion', which is often incorporated with pure negative freedom as part of a single concept of negative freedom, and 'autonomy' – are widely taken to be forms of liberty and are in fact the forms that are chiefly being referred to in the liberal claims about community and liberty. (It is claimed, for example, that public opinion in a community coerces the individual, thereby diminishing his liberty, and that individual autonomy is, in Stanley Benn's words, 'an idea available only to a plural tradition', hence impossible in a small community.) Some of the claims that have been made about liberty and community are in fact concerned, not with liberty, but with the sense or feeling of being free, with the value of liberty, and with certain capacities and powers.

4.1 Pure negative freedom, freedom from coercion, and autonomy

'An individual is unfree if, and only if, his doing of any action is rendered impossible by the action of another individual. That is, the unfree individual is so because the particular action is *prevented* by another.'[2] This is Hillel Steiner's characterisation, but, as we shall see later, it does not yield all the inferences he draws out of it. For emphasis and to avoid misunderstanding I shall refer to liberty characterised in this way as *pure negative freedom*. (Not only is this, in my view, the only clearly defined notion of liberty; it is also the only account which does not conflate several different ideas, some of them opaque and indistinct, which it is useful and fruitful to separate. Other accounts of 'liberty' bring in notions of identity, self-expression, obligations, preferences, reasonable expectations, powers and capacities, and more besides. But this is an argument I do not need to pursue here.)

I emphasise that whether a person has pure negative freedom or not is independent of his preferences, and that for pure negative freedom the action is rendered not merely improbable but impossible. Furthermore, I do not think it is helpful to view pure negative freedom as standing at one end of a continuum or

[2] Hillel Steiner, 'Individual liberty'.

as the limiting value of a variable: to say, for example, that an agent is (negatively) unfree *to the extent that* he is not subject to deliberate or coercive interference by others. It is not the case that an ever-increasing amount of coercive interference eventually renders an action literally impossible or that impossibility is, as it were, necessarily the limiting point of a sequence of increasing amounts of whatever it is the absence of which is deemed to constitute negative freedom.

On this account of liberty, then, an individual is not made unfree if he is *coerced* (that is, if he complies with credible, substantial threats: see Section 1.3). Coercion has, I think, been taken by many writers (including Oppenheim, Weinstein, Benn, Peters, Feinberg and Day)[3] to make individuals unfree for two different kinds of reasons. The first accepts that liberty results only from prevention but it is then argued that a threat does in fact prevent – render impossible – a certain action: if I am threatened by a highwayman in the usual way, I am (according to Day) rendered unable to do something I could otherwise have done, namely both have my money and also have my life, or rather I am made 'about to be' unable. This is a bizarre argument, for several reasons, one of which is especially relevant to one of the arguments I shall later make about the relation between community and liberty. Even when a threat is carried out, it need not (as Day supposes) diminish an individual's (pure negative) freedom, because the sanction associated with

[3] Felix E. Oppenheim, *Dimensions of Freedom* (New York: St Martin's Press, 1961); W. L. Weinstein, 'The concept of liberty in nineteenth century English political thought', *Political Studies*, 13 (1963), 145–62; S. I. Benn and W. L. Weinstein, 'Being free to act, and being a free man', *Mind*, 80 (1971), 194–211; R. S. Peters, 'Freedom and the development of the free man', in J. F. Doyle, ed., *Educational Judgements: Papers in the Philosophy of Education* (London: Routledge and Kegan Paul, 1973); Joel Feinberg, *Social Philosophy* (Englewood Cliffs, NJ: Prentice-Hall, 1973); S. I. Benn, 'Freedom, autonomy and the concept of a person', *Proceedings of the Aristotelian Society*, NS, 76 (1975–6), 109–30; J. P. Day, 'Threats, offers, law, opinion and liberty', *American Philosophical Quarterly*, 14 (1977), 257–72.

the threat need not render any action impossible. For example, the sanctions associated with a class of (usually tacit) threats which plays an important part in maintaining social order in primitive, peasant and some other communities do nothing more (or less) than damage the individual's public reputation and shame him, which does not in itself *prevent* him from *doing* anything (though if his reputation sinks sufficiently low it may *then* be impossible for him to do certain things – but that would be the result of the carrying out of a further tacit threat). The (good and bad) opinions of people you care about, or have to get on with, are everywhere powerful (positive and negative) sanctions but they do not in themselves make actions impossible; even if a threat to apply such sanctions were carried out, it would not restrict freedom. If the implementation of a threat does not necessarily make an individual unfree, then making the threat does not necessarily make an individual 'about to be' unfree.

On Day's account it is what *will* happen to the threatened individual, should he not comply, which renders him unfree when the threat is made: a trivial threat to twist my arm if I don't hand over my fortune makes me unfree, provided that you will implement the threat if I do not comply. Even though, as seems likely, this threat fails to induce me to comply, it is nevertheless deemed to have restricted my freedom just as surely as a non-trivial threat which *does* get me to do something I otherwise would not have done (and which would have been carried out if I had not complied); whereas a credible threat with which I in fact comply does *not* affect my freedom if you would have been prevented from carrying out the threat (although intending and able to) had I not complied. These are odd results, to say the least.

Threats, then, do not themselves restrict pure negative freedom. It is the imposition of sanctions, if and when the threat is carried out, which *may* diminish freedom.

Those other writers for whom coercion restricts liberty

usually view coercion and strict prevention as distinct modes of intervention: liberty consists in the absence of prevention *and* coercion.[4] And of these writers, some argue that the 'coercion' which limits liberty includes only threats (or certain kinds of threats) and others that it includes both threats and offers (of certain kinds).[5] But I have argued that neither threats nor offers, however great the associated penalties or rewards, render actions *impossible*, so do not restrict pure negative freedom; and in Section 1.3 I argued that 'coercion' should be restricted to the successful making of credible, substantial threats. The question that remains, then, is whether coercive threats should be viewed as curtailing some other sort of freedom.

The reason why coercion has been thought to restrict liberty (aside from Day's argument or any other argument to the effect that it renders the doing of some action impossible) is presumably that it is deemed in some circumstances to make the compliant action certain or 'virtually' certain or to constitute a 'sufficient causal condition' of it, or something of the sort. Now there are many ways, besides threats, in which one individual may get another to do something he would not otherwise have done by affecting his practical deliberations. Making offers is one such way, of course. Also, in many situations of interdependent decision-making, an individual may (perhaps intentionally) induce another to act differently merely by giving him sufficient reason to believe that he himself will choose a particular course of action, which need not correspond to imposing positive or negative sanctions contingently upon the other's behaviour. (He changes the other's beliefs, not his (expected) utilities.)[6] Or an individual may get another to do something he would not otherwise have done by providing information and arguments

---

[4] Some writers, however, take 'prevention' to include coercion, provided that the sanctions are sufficiently severe, and at least one of them (Feinberg) deems 'coercion' to include prevention.

[5] See the review in the first paragraph of Day, 'Threats, offers'.

about the nature of the choice alternatives, about the consequences of adopting different courses of action and the costs
and benefits attached to them – in other words by persuasion.
Any of these methods *could* amount to a 'sufficient causal
condition' of the 'compliant' action, could be said to make it
virtually certain, could be such as to enable an observer to
predict with considerable confidence that the compliant course
of action will be followed – *given*, of course, certain characteristics
of the object individual and his situation. Why, then, should
coercive threats be singled out from this range of 'compelling'
influences on the individual as the only ones which can be said
to limit his freedom? A possible answer is that a rational
individual would prefer not to be the recipient of a threat and
after a threat had been made he would prefer to be back in the
pre-threat situation, whereas he would not normally be averse
to (and would often positively welcome) interventions of the
other kinds mentioned, or at least he would not *regret* having
been subject to such interventions. It was on this criterion that
offers were deemed (in Section 1.3) not to be coercive; a
rational individual would normally not be averse to having
offers proposed to him. But the application of this criterion
would not leave the field to coercive threats alone.

While it can never strictly be said (as it often is) that coercion
leaves its victims 'no alternative' but to comply, there may be
circumstances in which the victim entirely lacks the ability or
capacity not to submit – as when 'the threat appeals to desires
or motives which are beyond the victim's ability to control'.[7]

---

[6] *Pace* Day, threats *do* affect the recipient's utilities – his *expected* utilities. Day
and many others are led astray by their failure to distinguish the courses of
action open to an individual in a situation of interdependent decision-
making and the *outcomes* of such decision-making, which of course generally
depend on the actions taken by all participants. A threat does not alter an
individual's preferences among outcomes (properly defined) but it does alter
the expected utility associated with each of the courses of action available to
him and it does this by changing his expectations about the actions to be
taken by others.

But then it would seem that the source of the individual's alleged unfreedom lies in his own dispositions as much as, or rather more than, the intervention of a threat.

There are, then, difficulties associated with the view that coercion restricts liberty, but they are not (and cannot be) conclusive reasons for rejecting it, and since 'freedom from coercion' (as I'll call it for want of a suitable expression that hasn't been expropriated for other uses), or a concept of negative freedom encompassing both pure negative freedom and freedom from coercion, is one of the forms of liberty which are the subject of claims about the incompatibility of community and liberty, I shall treat the absence of coercion as a form of liberty when I come to consider those claims.

I suggested earlier that the individual who complies with a threat because it 'appeals to desires or motives which are beyond the victim's ability to control' could be said to lack the *ability* to resist the threats. Abilities are not to be confused with freedoms, though to have the ability to do something may make the freedom to do it a more valuable one. To be moved by compulsive desires or more generally to be 'inner-impelled' is not to lack (some form of) liberty, as some writers claim; it is to lack certain abilities. These include, in Stanley Benn's well-known account, the capacities for making decisions and acting in accordance with them, for making and changing decisions and policies in the light of one's beliefs and of appropriate evidence, for 'formulating a project or policy so that a decision can be taken now for the sake of a preferred future state'.[8] Benn asserts (dubiously, in my view) that these capacities are a condition of being 'normal'; persons labelled as compulsive-obsessive, psychopathic, paranoid or schizophrenic are said to lack one or more of them. To possess these capacities is to be

---

[7] Harry G. Frankfurt, 'Coercion and moral responsibility'.
[8] Benn, 'Freedom, autonomy and the concept of a person'.

autarchic, but an individual is heterarchic only if these capacities have been impaired by someone else. Persons who are brainwashed (in a strong sense) or are acting under hypnosis or are 'unable to contemplate disobeying an authoritarian parent' are examples of heterarchy.

To lack abilities, even if this has been brought about intentionally by another person, is not to be unfree. In any case, I do not think that any general argument can be made about whether community is inimical to autarchy (although there is probably some relevant empirical evidence – which I haven't seen – on the incidence of the 'abnormalities', in and out of communities, which would disqualify a person from being autarchic).

The commonest liberal claim about the incompatibility of community and liberty concerns the putative form of liberty know as *autonomy*. The first problem confronting any attempt to deal with this claim is that (so far as I can see) no clear account of the concept of autonomy is available. It is generally agreed that two things are involved: rationality (having and using capacities of the kind mentioned in the last paragraph) and something often called authenticity. A person who acts on the results of rational deliberation may yet have wants and needs, subscribe to norms and principles, and lead a way of life, which he has taken over uncritically from his social milieu or which are provided for him ready-made by his social roles – which are not, in a word, 'his own' – and in this case he is said to lack authenticity. But if a person's wants, principles, and so on are not simply provided for him by others (as of course they must be to some extent), how do they arise? What does it mean to say that they are 'his own'? Two sorts of answers have been provided. The first is to say that an individual's thoughts or actions are authentic if they are an expression of his 'core self', which is defined as something like 'that constellation of relatively deeply rooted, important dispositions, knowledge of which helps us to anticipate and explain his actions over a relatively extended stretch of his total behaviour'.[9] If such anticipation and explanation is to be possible, it should be added that these basic dispositions must cohere; if they do not, the person lacks a 'core self'. An individual's thoughts and actions, on this account, are 'his own', when they are 'character-istic', or consistent with his 'nature' (though the same thoughts and actions might be characteristic of many other individuals).

This does, I think, catch one common use of 'authentic'. But if autonomy is to be counted as a form of liberty, then this account of authenticity will not suffice, for it makes no reference to the *source* of the 'deeply rooted dispositions' which make up the individual's 'character'. (What is more, authenticity in this sense seems a reasonable description of the behaviour of (non-human) animals, as some recent ethnological studies bring out quite clearly. I suspect that those who view autonomy as a (human) ideal would not be happy with this.)[10]

If autonomy is to be counted a form of liberty, the expression 'his own' has to carry more weight than this. The second approach to 'authenticity' tries to do this by saying that a person's wants, principles, etc., are 'his own' when they have been adopted or affirmed critically; when his actions are expressive of a character he has chosen to become or affirm as one he 'identifies' with; when he plays his roles critically, with distance. The life of an autonomous man, in Stanley Benn's

---

[9] Arnold S. Kaufman, 'Comments on Frankena's "The concept of education today"', in Doyle, ed., *Educational Judgements*.

[10] Mary Midgley writes of social animal species in *Beast and Man* (London: Methuen, 1980, ch. 11) that 'Each member has complex social ties, and develops them according to its character; the conventions are well understood, and *action contrary to the nature* either of the individual or the species can be easily spotted by the experienced observer. It shows up as something wrong ... something, as [Bishop] Butler said, "disproportionate to their nature as a whole".' Behaviour is 'not mechanical but purposive, and the purpose is linked to lasting character traits expressing priorities'.

words, 'has a consistency that derives from a coherent set of beliefs, values, and principles, by which his actions are governed' and 'these are not supplied to him ready-made as are those of the heteronomous man: they are *his*, because the outcome of a still-continuing process of criticism and re-valuation'. He does not simply accept 'the roles society thrusts on him, uncritically internalising the received *mores*', but is 'committed to a critical and creative search for coherence'.[11]

Autonomy in this sense is, in the view of several writers, a form of liberty, indeed the fundamental form. I might share this view if it could be shown that the critical choosing activity central to this conception of autonomy does not itself have causal determinants which are, in the words of Martin Hollis, 'external to the agent-*an-sich*'; but I doubt that this can be done.[12] Nevertheless, when I come to discuss the relations between liberty and community, I shall consider this notion of autonomy, since it is roughly what is being referred to in many of the claims about the incompatibility of community and liberty.

4.2 Are community and liberty incompatible?

An attempt to answer this question faces at the outset a problem about comparisons. The problem concerns the difficulty of comparing the overall freedom of one individual with that of another and the resulting difficulty of comparing the overall or 'on balance' freedom of one set of people with that of another. Recall that an agent possesses pure negative freedom with respect to an action if the action is not prevented, that is to say, rendered impossible, by the actions of other individuals. If

---

[11] Benn, 'Freedom, autonomy and the concept of a person'.
[12] Martin Hollis, *Models of Man* (Cambridge: Cambridge University Press, 1977). See also Hollis, 'Rational man and social science', in R. Harrison, ed., *Rational Action* (Cambridge: Cambridge University Press, 1979).

an individual is locked in a bare gaol cell (to follow Steiner's examples),[13] there is an indefinitely long list of actions he is not prevented from doing. Suppose next that he is locked inside a mummy case, itself inside the gaol cell. Presumably the list of prevented actions would lengthen and the list of unprevented actions would shorten. Yet there would be actions available to him now which were impossible before – 'rubbing his foot against the inside of the mummy case', for example. Thus, since we could never list *all* an individual's prevented and unprevented actions in any situation, these two situations cannot be conclusively compared with respect to the extent of pure negative freedom in them. But compare the situation in which the individual is locked in a cell containing an unlocked mummy case which he can lock from the inside with the situation in which he is locked (in the cell) inside a mummy case not lockable/unlockable from inside. Clearly, he is subject to less prevention in the first situation than in the second, and this is because all the actions available to him in the second situation, as well as other actions not available to him in that situation, are available to him in the first situation.

It is only of comparisons such as these – where the actions available to one individual are a *subset* of those available to another individual – that it could unequivocally be said that an individual had more pure negative freedom than another. To this it might be retorted that the actions available to the person locked inside a mummy case are trivial, unimportant, of no value to the imprisoned individual. Most people would agree; but the individual is nevertheless free to do these things, and in comparisons of the sort I'm interested in here no such presumptions about the unimportance of available actions can safely be made. If, for example, a person abandons a rich and varied life in the metropolis and enters an austere backwoods

[13] Steiner, 'Individual liberty'.

intentional community, many actions become available to him which previously were not. In *his* estimation some of these new opportunities may be highly valued. (Presumably, it is precisely because some of the actions available only in intentional communities are relatively highly valued that an individual would choose to enter or help to form one.) Generally speaking, comparisons of the overall or aggregate (subjective) utility or value of all the things that two individuals are free to do would be impossible. Only in simple cases (for example, the individual in the locked mummy case compared with almost anyone else) would it be possible to say that the aggregate value of the available actions was greater for one individual than for another.

So the retort, which in any case concerns the value of freedom rather than freedom itself, is not persuasive, and we are left with the result that comparisons of overall pure negative freedom are possible only where the actions available to one individual are a subset of those available to the other. This result, as we shall see, limits our ability to give a conclusive answer to the question whether community is inimical to pure negative freedom.

I begin this examination of the compatibility of community and liberty by discussing the effects on pure negative freedom of the practice of reciprocity. I cannot see any systematic relation between pure negative freedom and the other two criteria for community. (I do not, for example, think that shared values and beliefs – even with very considerable consensus – must *necessarily* reduce the occasions for and the use of force. Small, enclosed communities *are* generally much more pacific than, say, modern cities, but this is not the result of the greater similarity of beliefs and values.)

An agent has pure negative freedom with respect to an action if the action is not prevented – rendered impossible – by the action of another individual. Now 'to act is, among other things, to occupy particular portions of physical space and to dispose of particular material objects including, in the first instance, parts of one's own body', and if, following Steiner, we call the portions of physical space occupied and the materials disposed of, 'the physical components' of the action, it follows that 'to be free to do A . . . entails that all of the physical components of doing A are (simultaneously) unoccupied and/or undisposed of by another'.[14] This inference is correct; but, assuming that to occupy portions of physical space or to dispose of material objects is to *possess* them, Steiner's further inference, that *'freedom is the personal possession of physical objects'*, is incorrect, as is his deduction of a sort of law of conservation of freedom to the effect that a gain in freedom for an individual entails a corresponding loss of freedom for one or more others. It is true that while one individual has possession – enjoys exclusive physical control – of an object, possession during that time is denied to all others. But it does not follow that an individual possesses an object *if* nobody else does. Steiner's error was to assume tacitly that at any moment every object is in *somebody's* possession. An individual (on Steiner's own account) has pure negative freedom with respect to an action just as long as nobody else has possession of the physical components of that action; pure negative freedom does not require that *he* possesses these components. I am free at this moment, and at most times, to perform a variety of acts on the open fields I can see from my window, because neither their legal owner nor any other person has at this moment exclusive physical control of them (of the ground, of the air space directly above them, of the cabbages and corn and other objects on and in them). Of course, if I exercised this freedom – if I actually performed one of the acts I am free to do – then I would be in possession of

<hr>

[14] Steiner, 'Individual liberty', p. 47.

certain physical objects, so would *then* restrict the pure negative freedom of all other persons. But until I do so, they too have the relevant freedoms.

There is therefore no 'conservation of freedom'; it is not the case that 'within the universe of agents . . . there can be no such thing as an absolute loss of (or gain in) individual liberty'.[15] I have been at pains to deny this conclusion of Steiner's, by showing that freedom is *not* the possession of physical objects, because it bears directly on the argument I wish to make about community and pure negative freedom. For I shall now argue that the pure negative freedom of each of the members of a group would be augmented if they introduced the practice of one of the forms of reciprocity (everything else remaining the same).

A part of this argument has, in effect, been made by G. A. Cohen. Consider, he says, two neighbours A and B each of whom owns a set of household tools including some which the other lacks. 'If A needs a tool of a kind which only B has, then, private property being what it is, he is not free to take B's one for a while, even if B does not need it during that while.' But now, says Cohen, suppose that the two neighbours agree to share the tools which they do not both possess, according to this rule: 'each may take and use a tool belonging to the other without permission provided that the other is not using it and that he returns it when he no longer needs it, or when the other needs it, whichever comes first'.[16] Before the introduction of this sharing arrangement, which is a form of reciprocity, each individual at any point in time has pure negative freedom with respect to those actions requiring use of his own tool but lacks pure negative freedom with respect to those actions requiring use of the other individual's tool. After the arrangement is

---

[15] Steiner, 'Individual liberty', pp. 49–50.
[16] G. A. Cohen, 'Capitalism, freedom and the proletariat', in A. Ryan, ed., *The Idea of Freedom* (Oxford: Oxford University Press, 1979).

introduced each participant is free all of the time to do the first class of actions (because his use of his own tool cannot be blocked by his neighbour, who must return it on demand) *and* is now free to do the second class of actions during all the time that the other participant is not using his own tool. The only qualification which the first half of this statement might require is that each individual is not free to use his tool during the time it takes for it to be returned to him by his neighbour (this is the 'inconvenience' of the arrangement). If this, usually trivial, diminution of freedom is set aside, it can be said that the introduction of this particular form of reciprocity augments the pure negative freedom of each participant. Of course, if one of the 'participants' uses his own tool *all* the time, the other's freedom is not augmented; but nor is it diminished.

A person could have a bilateral sharing arrangement of this kind with many other persons. If the same tool is the subject of several bilateral arrangements, then the rule would specify that the tool is available to any individual only when nobody else is using it and that it is returned to its owner when not in use or as soon as its owner needs it. Obviously, if a tool is much in demand, an individual (other than the owner) might have to wait some time before the tool is available for his use; but provided that tools sometimes become available to him which were not available before and the inconvenience involved in retrieving his own tools when needed is not great, this multilateral arrangement also augments the pure negative freedom of each participant.

Can an argument of this sort be applied to other forms of reciprocity? Consider the case of reciprocal giving, where the reciprocity is of the generalised kind, the recipient of a gift having only a diffuse obligation to make a return gift which need not be in kind, or of exactly the same value, or made immediately. Food sharing, common in primitive societies, is an example. In hunting and gathering bands, a man who kills a large animal would share it with others, expecting to benefit similarly when others are successful in the hunt. A less palaeolithic example is the reciprocal giving of produce; A gives B eggs when he has a surplus and receives from B some of his surplus tomatoes. This form of reciprocity, however, differs from the tool sharing sort in that the objects involved in the reciprocal giving remain under the exclusive control of their owner before they are given and under the exclusive control of the recipient afterwards. The result is that reciprocal giving involves a *trading* of freedoms to do *dated* acts. Individual A (an Eskimo) trades the freedom to gorge himself on a whole seal at t_1 and (to give a more philosophical example) the freedom to swing the carcase around his head at t_2, and so on, in exchange for the freedom to eat (or do other things with) portions of seal at other times; or he trades the freedom to throw his surplus tomatoes at his garden wall (and to do an infinity of other things with them) in exchange for the freedom to dispose of the surplus eggs given him at other times. So it cannot be said that this form of reciprocity augments the pure negative freedom of the participants *or* that it diminishes it.

It is, however, true that such reciprocity, as it is typically practised in communities, does increase each participant's utility, because typically what is given is what is not then needed or cannot then be used, and what is received is of more value, so that the freedoms lost are less valuable than those gained.

The third type of reciprocity which is widely practised in communities takes the form of cooperative work, labour pooling or reciprocal assistance. I'll refer to it here as cooperation. Examples are: participation in cooperative hunting; contributing to communal projects such as irrigation schemes, the erection of public buildings, and so on; help with private house re-building and especially with things which need to be done faster than the individual or household can manage alone, like planting or harvesting a crop. Despite its superficial similarity to the first form of reciprocity (when a person pools his labour he makes it available to others, just as the tool-sharer makes his tool available to others), cooperation cannot be assimilated to it. Cooperation does not make a person free to do things he was previously unfree to do. Without cooperation, he is unable to catch large game or to re-build his house alone or to harvest his crop before the rains come. But cooperation does not render him free to do these things; it makes the cooperators *jointly* capable of doing them *together*. So A, when not helping or cooperating with B, does not withhold something from B control of which would enable *B* to perform some action. So the pure negative freedom of participating individuals is neither augmented nor diminished by this form of reciprocity. This result does not imply that the *utility* of the participants is not increased by cooperation; in general, presumably, it is.

Summarising this discussion of reciprocity and pure negative freedom, we can say that of the three important forms of reciprocity one augments the freedom of the participants while the other two cannot be shown to diminish it.

A great deal of reciprocity in communities, even though it is generalised in spirit, is in practice roughly balanced in the long run – everyone contributes about the same amount of resources. But some generalised reciprocity – especially in primitive and peasant communities – does not balance out. We saw in Chapter 3 that the practice of generalised reciprocity is one of several levelling practices found very widely in stateless primitive societies, in peasant communities of the closed corporate kind, and in some other communities. Indeed, I argued in that chapter that community requires a rough economic equality among its members and that this equality can be maintained in community. Clearly, an approximate economic equality helps, other things being equal, to undermine an important basis of coercion. But it does not by any means remove all opportunities for coercion, for the methods of social control characteristic of community can be coercive.

There are two kinds of social control which are used in *all* communities for the maintenance of both social order and a rough economic equality. They ought therefore to enter into any evaluation of the prospects for freedom in community. Both kinds of control employ threats. The first threatens (*via* gossip, ridiculing, etc.) shame, damage to one's public reputation, and so on. The second threatens withdrawal of some or all of the benefits of reciprocity. As we have seen, making threats, even coercive threats, does not in itself restrict pure negative freedom. But the imposition of sanctions, if and when a threat is carried out (and threats are unlikely to remain credible if they are not carried out from time to time), *may* diminish pure negative freedom. Carrying out a threat of the first kind does *not* diminish pure negative freedom because the sanction does not render any action impossible: shaming an individual or damaging his public reputation does not in itself prevent him from doing anything. As for the second kind of social control, since I have already argued that only one form of reciprocity clearly augments the pure negative freedom of each participant, it follows trivially that carrying out the threat to withdraw this form of reciprocity diminishes pure negative freedom; but this cannot be said of the other forms of reciprocity.

What of 'freedom from coercion'? To what extent is this curtailed by these two kinds of social control? It is difficult to answer this in the abstract. Whether the sanctions associated with the second kind of threat are sufficiently substantial to be coercive depends in part on the circumstances of the individual in question. In many situations the withdrawal of some forms of reciprocal giving and cooperation is a very dire sanction indeed. The sanctions associated with threats of the first kind (shaming, etc.) are generally less severe but are nevertheless widely feared in the (small, stable) community, as I've emphasised in earlier chapters. The members of communities, then, are not free from coercion.

Nor, of course, are people who do not live in communities. The social controls characteristic of societies with states make use of threats which are often coercive and which limit pure negative freedom when carried out. Furthermore, the subjects of a state are likely to *feel* less free from coercion, and to feel more frustrated and dissatisfied, than the members of a community, because there is less *participation* in collective decision-making and in the processes of social control in states than in communities (see Section 3.1).

This is perhaps the appropriate place to say a parenthetical word about *privacy*. Privacy, it may be thought, is something that has to be sacrificed in a community, and its absence is a form of unfreedom. The second part of this claim is mistaken. Privacy is in itself not a form of liberty, though public exposure of certain aspects of behaviour facilitates (and is enhanced by) the operation of the social controls characteristic of community, which may be coercive, as we have seen. As for the first part of the claim, there is no doubt that in *some* communities – in some primitive societies and in some intentional communities – there is much less privacy than is typically found in modern industrial societies, for example. But in fact community *requires* privacy to be invaded only to the extent necessary for relations between people to be direct and many-sided and for the social controls characteristic of community to be effective. If an individual deals with others directly and many-sidedly, then clearly more is likely to be known about him than in a society in which relations in many areas are mediated or specialised. And of course carrying out the threats associated with the social controls, especially the use of gossip, ridicule, and so on, makes the individual's delicts and defaults much more widely known than is often the case with the application of sanctions in 'mass' societies. But this widespread public knowledge of *some* aspects of an individual's behaviour clearly does not entail a general lack of privacy, a wholly exposed life lived constantly in public view.

Although I was unable to give a very clear account of the concept of autonomy, I shall nevertheless try now to see what I can make of the claim that autonomy is incompatible with community, being 'an ideal available only to a plural tradition' (Benn). My tentative conclusion is that the second part of this statement is trivially correct, but that this implies neither the truth of the first part nor that autonomy is often actually achieved in plural societies. I shall need, obviously, to distinguish between communities which are decidedly un-plural and those in which, even though a diversity of fundamentally different lifestyles may not exist side by side, alternative roles, identities, values and beliefs are accessible.

For autonomy to be an 'available ideal', the individual must have the capacities and inclination for subjecting his values and beliefs, norms and principles to critical scrutiny, he must be able to make out of this critical process a coherent set of values, beliefs, etc., and he must be able to choose or to create (with the cooperation of others) an appropriate role or character with which he 'identifies'. Clearly, these processes and choices are conceivable only in a pluralist society. But it is not at all obvious that this requires, as some writers suppose, a society in which a very great diversity of values, beliefs and lifestyles co-exist and that the individual must be aware of and expose himself to these alternative ways of thinking and living. Leaving aside the possibility that such great diversity is dependent on a considerable degree of economic inequality (which is incompatible with community), there is no general reason why, faced with such a diversity, more than a very few individuals would be able to succeed in securing their identity in the way required for autonomy. They are just as likely to wander perpetually in this 'pluralisation of life-worlds' with what Peter Berger has called a 'homeless mind': 'Put differently, there is a built-in identity crisis in the contemporary situation',[17] and an identity crisis is what I have 'when what I am no longer accounts for who I am, because what I do is no longer the rational acting out of what I have chosen to become';[18] in other words when I have failed to achieve autonomy.

Autonomy is a possibility in a plural society, but it is also a problem. For the members of primitive and peasant communities it is not a problem; they feel at home in a coherent world and do not have to work hard for a sense of identity. But knowing who you are, or rather what you are, is not the same thing as being autonomous; feeling free is not being free. If the individual in such a society is not autonomous, however, it is not because he is a slave to tradition, a perfectly socialised, infallible conformer to his community's norms; there is plenty of deviance here. He's neither the obedient citizen nor the gung ho free rider. Nor yet is he the autonomous man in the middle.[19] Autonomy is just not a possibility for him.

Are there, then, any communities in which some measure of autonomy can be achieved? I think there are. The strongest contender is what Abrams and McCulloch call the 'secular family commune', the dominant form in the present wave of commune activity.[20] It is crucial to distinguish this form from the 'utopian community' which was the dominant form in the nineteenth-century waves of commune building, especially in America, though there are many examples in the current phase

---

[17] Peter L. Berger, Brigitte Berger and Hansfried Kellner, *The Homeless Mind* (New York: Random House, 1973).
[18] Hollis, *Models of Man*, p. 106.
[19] Cf. Hollis, 'Rational man and social science'.
[20] Philip Abrams and Andrew McCulloch, *Communes, Sociology and Society*. The following discussion of intentional community owes much to this excellent work as well as drawing on what I have learned from hundreds of hours of conversations with secular family commune members.

too. The secular family commune is probably unique in the degree to which community and autonomy are *together* valued, sought after, and in some instances successfully achieved in practice. For this reason, we can learn much about the compatibility of autonomy and community from the experience of these communes and from study of what it is about other varieties of intentional community which is inimical to autonomy.

The sort of communes which Abrams and McCulloch call secular family communes are 'groups devoted to communal living for its own sake as a way of institutionalising friendship within and around a chosen domestic place'. Now friendship (see Section 1.4 above) is in any case a precarious relationship. It is (in the words of Abrams and McCulloch) 'threatened to the extent that the parties to a relationship [are] moved by utilitarian or hedonistic motives; . . . threatened to the extent that their own selves [are] insecure; and . . . threatened to the extent that their statuses [are] unequal'. But the attempt to institutionalise friendship on the basis of place-making is further beset by 'the danger of treating the activity through which friendship is cemented and achieved as an end in itself and more important than the relationship or individuals that it is expressing',[21] of concentrating on place-making *per se* to such an extent that it displaces friendship as the point of the commune. This is an example of the danger of *reification*.

Reification in a number of forms obstructs not just friendship (which is an important characteristic of this kind of community but not of most others) but also one of the three central characteristics of community. The commitment of the community's members to an ideology, religious or secular, to an abstract idea of the community, *mediates* the relations between them; they relate to *it*, rather than directly to each other; and in some degree they subordinate themselves to it. It is also

[21] Abrams and McCulloch, *Communes, Sociology and Society*, p. 30.

inimical to individual autonomy. For it provides a framework for thought and action, perhaps even an explicit detailed code regulating their behaviour. To the extent that such reification is joined to a strong commitment of members to the community and its ideology, to that extent also is autonomy blocked. For the members of such a community, the spirit of critical evaluation which is characteristic of autonomy is stunted, and the individual is hardly encouraged to experiment with different activities and social relations and roles, or to develop his capacities and faculties, unless these happen to be congruent with the ideology and organisation of the community.

Reification, strong commitment, self-denial and submersion of the self in the community are characteristic of the utopian community. These communities generally have strong leadership (usually charismatic) as well as an explicit ideology (usually religious) and often a detailed code of conduct, all of which mediate relations between members. Such are the well-known religious communities of the Hutterites, the Shakers, the Bruderhof, the Oneida community of Perfectionists, and many others, and utopian communities based on social and economic ideologies such as those founded on the ideas of Owen, Fourier and Cabet (though in some of the latter group 'subordination' was the founders' ideal but not the members' practice).[22]

---

[22] Two of the better books on utopian communities *of this sort* are R. M. Kanter, *Commitment and Community* and Benjamin Zablocki, *The Joyful Community: An Account of the Bruderhof, a Communal Movement Now in its Third Generation* (Baltimore: Penguin, 1971). However, neither of these studies throws much light on the problems of the secular family commune or on the problem of the compatibility of freedom and community. Kanter concentrates her attention on problems of commitment and self-denial, which, important though they undoubtedly are in the study of utopian communities, provide a misleading focus for looking at modern secular communes; indeed she fails to see that some of her 'mechanisms of commitment' to community (communion, sacrifice, investment, renunciation, mortification and transcendence) are to some extent *destructive* of community. Zablocki, who asserts at the end of his book that 'conflict between community and freedom' is 'a theme that has run implicitly through (the) book', appears to see this conflict as one of 'self' *versus* 'Society'.

The utopian 'community' provides a ready-made *nomos* for its members. But since these communities are always islands within, or on the frontier fringes of, the larger society, and are, to a greater or lesser extent, maintained by recruitment from that society, their members bring with them into the community the memory of, and afterwards are occasionally exposed to, beliefs, values, principles, norms and ways of living alternative to those of the community. Furthermore, it is always open to them to leave the community. Thus, although the *nomos* is largely ready-made for them, it is for most members one which is *chosen*, is identified with, and can be rejected. And this is scarcely true of the primitive societies and closed corporate peasant communities. Again, although most members may not live up to the ideal of the person engaged in a 'continuing process of criticism and evaluation', there is some criticism, of a kind barely possible in the primitive and peasant communities, and in some cases the whole community participates in rule making and modification. I conclude that there is limited scope for the achievement of a measure of autonomy in the utopian 'community', while emphasising that *it is precisely those things which limit autonomy which also limit the degree to which these utopias are truly communities.*

In the secular family commune, by contrast, there is an attempt to maintain direct relations, unmediated by reifications, by elaborate ideologies of what the community is about and accounts of how everyone ought to act; there is a more tentative acceptance of organisational forms and codes of behaviour, which are submitted to more critical evaluation and are modified by processes of mutual negotiation in which all participate as friends. To be sure, these features of the secular family commune are ideals; but many communes have gone a long way towards realising them in practice. They are all conducive to the achievement of autonomy.

It has not been my intention in this chapter to argue that liberty is maximised in, or is possible only in community. My discussion of the relation between community and liberty is radically incomplete but certainly suffices to show that this conclusion, which is almost an assumption in the writings of some communitarian anarchists, cannot be supported; but it also shows that the contrary claim, associated especially with liberal writers, that community is inimical to individual liberty, is equally unsupportable. If liberty is taken as a central value or ideal (though I do not argue in this book that it should be), the small community does not stand condemned.

5

Epilogue: the future of community and anarchy

Anarchy is viable to the extent that the relations between people are those which are characteristic of community. In a community, social order can be maintained without the state; so too can the approximate economic equality which community requires. So that, insofar as community was shown in the last chapter to be not incompatible with individual liberty, it can be said, contrary to the claims of liberal writers, that the principal ideals of communitarian anarchists (and of some other socialists), namely anarchy, liberty, equality and community, form a coherent set.

As they stand, the arguments I have used apply to a single community in isolation, to its internal relations. But what of the relations between communities, between a community and the rest of the world? Do not some of the problems of anarchy, which can be 'solved' by the egalitarian community internally, reappear in the relations *between* communities? If, in the absence of the state, behaviour destructive of social order and behaviour tending to promote economic inequality can be inhibited and contained between individuals because they are co-members of a community, what is to control such behaviour between people who are not of the same community? It would appear to be an implication of the argument in Chapter 2 that, in a world constituted of communities, order and a rough material equality among communities can be maintained insofar as the relations *between* communities are those characteristic of community, unless the communities themselves are to be subject to an inter-communal state. But communities are necessarily small, and 'universal community' impossible. The controls which can be effective within the small community cannot generally have a great impact on relations between people of different communities.

Communitarian anarchist writers themselves have not seen any great problem here. But then generally speaking they have not recognised that there would be a social order problem *within* the small community. The classical anarchist writers saw the key to relations between the various small units they envisaged (communities, communes, associations of workers) to be some variant of federalism. The units were to have considerable autonomy, but coordination, cooperation, exchange, the settling of disputes and perhaps redistribution would require them to confederate, at least some of the time. The federations, between the smallest units and between confederations of them, were of course to be voluntary. Where necessary, the communities would send delegates to assemblies, the delegates to be recallable, part-time non-professionals, the assemblies to meet *ad hoc* perhaps, to be strictly limited in their sphere of operations, certainly never to have their decisions backed up by great concentrations of force. Confederal relations between communities, like relations between members of the same community, would be 'fraternal'.

Even if all the world were made up of genuine communities, this vision of voluntary confederal relations among them is as over-optimistic as the anarchists' expectations that social order within the community would present no very great problem. We have no grounds for believing that growing up and living in a community necessarily engenders a tolerant, pacific and cooperative disposition towards outsiders. It is true that many primitive anarchic communities lived at peace with their neighbours (though having little contact with them and invariably taking a dim view of them); but many did not, and the world is a great deal more crowded now.

I have not seen a plausible solution to this problem of inter-communal relations in the literature of anarchism or anywhere else, and I do not have a solution which I find persuasive myself. But it should be remembered that the problem is altogether less severe than that of the relations between nations, for there is the fundamental difference that the communities we are talking about would be stateless as well as small, so that the potential for inter-communal aggression and exploitation would be limited. In view of this, the goal of a radically decentralised world of small communities is not rendered less attractive than the present state of affairs solely in virtue of the lack of a solution to the problem of inter-communal relations.

The *transition* to such a world of small anarchic communities is fraught with another problem, that of the relation between, on the one hand, communities and partial and quasi-communities (about which more in a moment) and, on the other hand, states, both 'foreign' states and those of which the budding communities are enclaves. We saw in Section 3.3 that nearly all states were 'secondary' formations, the direct or indirect result, at least in part, of the presence nearby of already existing states, and that the egalitarian anarchic community, though it can last for millennia if left alone, is terribly vulnerable to other states. Societies without a state were subjugated, colonised or absorbed by states, or became more politically centralised and militarily organised as a result of attacks or threats, real or imagined, or encroachment, actual or feared, by neighbouring states. This history of the vulnerability of the anarchic community in the face of societies with greater political centralisation and con-centration of force gives little ground for optimism about the survival and even the emergence of any substantial region of anarchic communities. How far the process of building small enclaves of quasi-anarchic community (such as the present communes) and developing various forms of partial community can go, it is difficult to say; but the prospects for a sweeping success seem not too bright unless the movement towards community and anarchy in any area or sphere, at least in its later stages, is simultaneously matched by similar movements everywhere.[1]

What, under modern conditions, does this movement towards anarchy and community consist in? It very roughly corresponds, I think, to what Martin Buber called 'structural renewal' or 'pre-revolutionary structure-making' – though I should like to include under this head a variety of developments which Buber does not mention in *Paths in Utopia*. (All of these developments are the subjects of a vast literature, past and current, so I shall do no more than indicate them briefly.) Structural renewal includes, in the first place, attempts to build whole communities – communes, *kibbutzim*, and so on. These will of course not be wholly anarchic, being to some degree subject to the states in which they are enclaves; and they will vary in the degree to which they approximate to true communities (recall, for example, the difference between the modern secular family commune and the 'utopian community' in which strong leadership and an explicit ideology, usually religious, mediate relations between members). I have discussed these intentional communities in earlier chapters.

But there is another line of development, perhaps more promising than the building of whole communities and certainly with very wide application, and this is the development of what might be called 'partial community', covering a wide variety of cooperatives, collectives, neighbourhood associations and other practices and projects of direct action, mutual aid and self-management. All of these (with an important qualification to be noted shortly) further the building of community and

---

[1] A similar conclusion is drawn (about 'true democratisation' via a long series of 'non-reformist reforms') by Theda Skocpol from her study of *States and Social Revolutions* (Cambridge: Cambridge University Press, 1979), p. 293.

directly or indirectly of anarchy too, by (i) fostering or deepening reciprocity; (ii) diminishing mediation and political specialisation by short-cutting the offices of the state and widening political participation; and (iii) in some cases stimulating or even necessitating less specialised relations between people.[2]

An important qualification must be made to this view of the role of cooperatives, collectives, self-management, and so on, in the process of community renewal. When a group of people form a cooperative, assume control of their workplace, establish a system of mutual assistance, or whatever, this action *in itself* makes *their* relations more like those of a community. But cooperation and self-management can serve many purposes. In particular, they can be used for purposes which indirectly are destructive of community, especially amongst people other than the cooperators. Certain products, for example, are almost bound to be used in ways which are damaging to community, and this effect is of course quite independent of whether they are produced in factories managed (or even owned) by the workers or by any sort of capitalist firm. This is certainly true of motor cars (which also generate inequality and diminish most people's, probably everyone's, freedom, as well as being a major source of pollution, having other baneful effects on the natural environment, and being colossally inefficient) and of nuclear energy, to take two obvious examples.[3]

Of course, there is no decrease in community when, say, workers' self-management is introduced into a car-producing firm which continues to produce the same quantity of the same product; there is, amongst the workers in question, some small

---

[2] Needless to say, the building of cooperatives, collectives, etc. and the practice of direct action, mutual aid and self-management generate effects other than those on community and anarchy which are my sole concern here. For some of their other effects and other grounds for their justification, see for example Carole Pateman, *Participation and Democratic Theory* (Cambridge: Cambridge University Press, 1970) and Tony Gibson, *People Power: Community and Work Groups in Action* (Harmondsworth: Penguin, 1979), Part I.

increase. My point is that self-management and other forms of cooperation and direct relations are not enough. From the point of view of the growth of community and indirectly of anarchy, the nature of the product of this cooperation is important too.

[3] See Ivan Illich, *Energy and Equity* (London: Calder and Boyars, 1974) and *Tools for Conviviality* (London: Calder and Boyars, 1973); Amory Lovins, *Soft Energy Paths* (Harmondsworth: Penguin, 1977), especially sec. 2.9 and ch. 9; Michael Flood and Robin Grove-White, *Nuclear Prospects: A Comment on the Individual, the State and Nuclear Power* (London: Friends of the Earth, 1976); André Gorz, *Ecology as Politics* (Boston: South End Press, 1980). Lovins argues that the hard energy path, of which nuclear fission is a central component, 'demands strongly interventionist central control . . . concentrates political and economic power . . . encourages urbanization . . . increases bureaucratization and alienation . . . is probably inimical to greater distributional equity within and between nations . . . inequitably divorces costs from benefits . . . enhances vulnerability and the paramilitarization of civilian life . . . and nurtures – even requires – elitist technocracy whose exercise erodes the legitimacy of democratic government' (*Soft Energy Paths*, p. 148).

Bibliography

Abrams, Philip, and McCulloch, Andrew. *Communes, Sociology and Society*. Cambridge: Cambridge University Press, 1976.

Adams, Robert McC. *The Evolution of Urban Society: Early Mesopotamia and Prehispanic Mexico*. Chicago: Aldine, 1966.

Arrow, Kenneth J. *Social Choice and Individual Values*. 2nd edition. New York: Wiley, 1963.

'Uncertainty and the economics of medical care', *American Economic Review*, 53 (1963), 941–73.

Bachrach, Peter, and Baratz, Morton S. *Power and Poverty*. New York: Oxford University Press, 1970.

Barry, Brian. *The Liberal Theory of Justice*. Oxford: Clarendon Press, 1973.

Review of Robert Nozick, *Anarchy, State and Utopia, Political Theory*, 3 (1975), 331–6.

'Power: an economic analysis', in B. Barry, ed., *Power and Political Theory: Some European Perspectives*. London: Wiley, 1976.

Baxter, Paul. 'Absence makes the heart grow fonder; some suggestions why witchcraft accusations are rare among East African pastoralists', in Max Gluckman, ed., *The Allocation of Responsibility*. Manchester: Manchester University Press, 1972.

Benn, S. I. 'Freedom, autonomy and the concept of a person', *Proceedings of the Aristotelian Society*, NS, 76 (1975–6), 109–30.

Benn, S. I., and Weinstein, W. L. 'Being free to act, and being a free man', *Mind*, 80 (1971), 194–211.

Berger, Peter L.; Berger, Brigitte; and Kellner, Hansfried. *The Homeless Mind*. New York: Random House, 1973.

Bernardo, Robert M. *The Theory of Moral Incentives in Cuba*. University, Alabama: University of Alabama Press, 1971.

Berndt, Ronald M. *Excess and Restraint: Social Control Among a New Guinea People*. Chicago: University of Chicago Press, 1962.

Birrell, R. J. 'The centralized control of the communes in the post-"Great Leap" period', in A. Doak Barnett, ed., *Chinese Communist Politics in Action*. Seattle: University of Washington Press, 1969.

Black, R. A. 'Hopi grievance chants: a mechanism of social control', in D. Hymes and W. E. Brittle, eds., *Studies in Southwestern Ethnolinguistics.* The Hague: Mouton, 1967.

Black-Michaud, Jacob. *Cohesive Force: Feud in the Mediterranean and the Middle East.* Oxford: Blackwell, 1975.

Blum, Jerome. *Lord and Peasant in Russia from the Ninth to the Nineteenth Century.* Princeton, NJ: Princeton University Press, 1961.

'The European village as community: origins and functions', *Agricultural History*, 45 (1971), 157–78.

'The internal structure and polity of the European village community from the fifteenth to the nineteenth century', *Journal of Modern History,* 43 (1971), 541–76.

Bohannan, Laura. 'Political aspects of Tiv social organization', in J. Middleton and D. Tait, eds., *Tribes Without Rulers.* London: Routledge and Kegan Paul, 1958.

Buber, Martin. *Paths in Utopia.* Boston: Beacon Press, 1958.

Carens, Joseph A. *Equality, Moral Incentives, and the Market: An Essay in Utopian Politico-Economic Theory.* Chicago: University of Chicago Press, 1981.

Carneiro, Robert L. 'A theory of the origin of the state', *Science,* 169 (1970), 733–8.

Chamberlin, John. 'Provision of collective goods as a function of group size', *American Political Science Review*, 68 (1974), 707–16.

Chambliss, William J., and Seidman, Robert B. *Law, Order and Power.* Reading, Mass.: Addison-Wesley, 1971.

Charlton, John. 'Political power', PhD dissertation, University of Essex, 1978.

Chayanov, A. V. *The Theory of Peasant Economy.* Homewood, Illinois: Richard D. Irwin, 1966.

Childe, V. Gordon. *Man Makes Himself.* London: Watts, 1936.

Claessen, Henri J. M., and Skalnik, Peter, eds., *The Early State.* The Hague: Mouton, 1978.

Cohen, G. A. 'Robert Nozick and Wilt Chamberlain: how patterns preserve liberty', in J. Arthur and W. H. Shaw, eds., *Justice and Economic Distribution.* Englewood Cliffs, NJ: Prentice-Hall, 1978.

'Capitalism, freedom and the proletariat', in A. Ryan, ed., *The Idea of Freedom.* Oxford: Oxford University Press, 1979.

Cohen, Ronald. 'The political system', in R. Naroll and R. Cohen, eds., *A Handbook of Method in Cultural Anthropology.* New York: Natural History Press, 1971.

'The natural history of hierarchy: a case study', in T. Burns and W. Buckley, eds., *Power and Control: Social Structures and their Transformation.* London and Beverly Hills: Sage, 1976.

'State origins: a reappraisal', in H. J. M. Claessen and P. Skalnik, eds., *The Early State*. The Hague: Mouton, 1978.

Cohen, Ronald, and Service, Elman R., eds. *Origins of the State: The Anthropology of Political Evolution*. Philadelphia: Institute for the Study of Human Issues, 1978.

Colson, Elizabeth. 'Social control and vengeance in Plateau Tonga society', *Africa*, 23 (1953), 199–212.

Culyer, A. J. *Need and the National Health Service*. London: Martin Robertson, 1976.

The Political Economy of Social Policy. Oxford: Martin Robertson, 1980.

Day, J. P. 'Threats, offers, law, opinion and liberty', *American Philosophical Quarterly*, 14 (1977), 257–72.

Demsetz, Harold. 'The private production of public goods', *Journal of Law and Economics,* 13 (1970), 293–306.

Douglas, Mary, ed. *Witchcraft Accusations and Confessions*. London: Tavistock, 1970.

Draper, Hilary. *Private Police*. Harmondsworth: Penguin, 1978.

Easton, David. 'Political anthropology', in B. J. Siegel, ed., *Biennial Review of Anthropology 1959*. Stanford: Stanford University Press, 1959.

Engels, Frederick. *The Origin of the Family, Private Property and the State*. London: Lawrence and Wishart, 1972.

Erasmus, Charles J. *In search of the Common Good: Utopian Experiments Past and Future*. New York: Free Press, 1977.

Evans-Pritchard, E. E. *The Nuer*. Oxford: Clarendon Press, 1940.

Farb, Peter. *Man's Rise to Civilisation as Shown by the Indians of North America from Primeval Times to the Coming of the Industrial State*. London: Paladin, 1971.

Feinberg, Joel. *Social Philosophy*. Englewood Cliffs, NJ: Prentice-Hall, 1973.

Firth, Raymond. *We, The Tikopia*. London: Allen and Unwin, 1936.

Economics of the New Zealand Maori. 2nd edition. Wellington, New Zealand: R. E. Owen, Government Printer, 1959.

Flannery, Kent V. 'The cultural evolution of civilizations', *Annual Review of Ecology and Systematics,* 3 (1972), 399–426.

Flood, Michael, and Grove-White, Robin. *Nuclear Prospects: A Comment on the Individual, the State and Nuclear Power*. London: Friends of the Earth, 1976.

Fortes, M. 'The political system of the Tallensi of the Northern Territories of the Gold Coast', in M. Fortes and E. E. Evans-Pritchard, eds., *African Political Systems*. London: Oxford University Press, 1940.

Fox, Robin. *Kinship and Marriage*. Harmondsworth: Penguin, 1967.

Frankfurt, Harry G. 'Coercion and moral responsibility', in T. Honderich, ed., *Essays on Freedom of Action*. London: Routledge and Kegan Paul, 1973.

Fried, Morton H. *The Evolution of Political Society*. New York: Random House, 1967.

Friedman, David. *The Machinery of Freedom: Guide to a Radical Capitalism*. New York: Harper and Row, 1973.

Friedrich, Carl. *Man and His Government*. New York: McGraw-Hill, 1963.

Tradition and Authority. London: Macmillan, 1972.

Fürer-Haimendorf, Christoph von. *Morals and Merit: A Study of Values and Social Controls in South Asian Societies*. London: Weidenfeld and Nicolson, 1967.

Gibson, Tony. *People Power: Community and Work Groups in Action*. Harmondsworth: Penguin, 1979.

Gintis, Herbert. 'A radical analysis of welfare economics and individual development', *Quarterly Journal of Economics*, 86 (1972), 572–99.

'Welfare criteria with endogenous preferences: the economics of education', *International Economic Review*, 15 (1974), 415–30.

Gluckman, Max. *Custom and Conflict in Africa*. Oxford: Blackwell, 1955.

Politics, Law and Ritual in Tribal Society. Oxford: Blackwell, 1977.

Gorz, André. *Ecology as Politics*. Boston: South End Press, 1980.

Hardin, Russell. *Collective Action*. Baltimore: Johns Hopkins University Press for Resources for the Future, 1982.

Harsanyi, John. 'Measurement of social power, opportunity costs, and the theory of two-person bargaining games' and 'Measurement of social power in *n*-person reciprocal power situations', *Behavioral Science*, 7 (1962), 67–92.

Hayek, Friedrich A. *Law, Legislation and Liberty*, vol. 2: *The Mirage of Social Justice*. Chicago: University of Chicago Press, 1976.

Hobsbawm, Eric. 'The idea of fraternity', *New Society*, 34 (27 November 1975), 471–3.

Hochman, H. H., and Rodgers, J. D. 'Pareto optimal redistribution', *American Economic Review*, 59 (1969), 542–57.

Hoffman, Charles. *Work Incentive Practices and Policies in the People's Republic of China 1953–1965*. Albany, NY: State University of New York Press, 1967.

The Chinese Worker. Albany, NY: State University of New York Press, 1974.

Hollis, Martin. *Models of Man*. Cambridge: Cambridge University Press, 1977.

'Rational man and social science', in R. Harrison, ed., *Rational Action*. Cambridge: Cambridge University Press, 1979.

Howe, Christopher. 'Labour organization and incentives in industry, before and after the Cultural Revolution', in Stuart Schram, ed., *Authority, Participation, and Cultural Change in China.* Cambridge: Cambridge University Press, 1973.

Illich, Ivan. *Tools for Conviviality.* London: Calder and Boyars, 1973. *Energy and Equity.* London: Calder and Boyars, 1974.

Kang, G. E. 'Conflicting loyalties theory: a cross-cultural test', *Ethnology,* 15 (1976), 201–10.

Kanter, Rosabeth Moss. *Commitment and Community: Communes and Utopias in Sociological Perspective.* Cambridge, Mass.: Harvard University Press, 1972.

Kaufman, Arnold S. 'Comments on Frankena's "The concept of education today"', in J. F. Doyle, ed., *Educational Judgements: Papers in the Philosophy of Education.* London: Routledge and Kegan Paul, 1973.

Krader, Lawrence. *Formation of the State.* Englewood Cliffs, NJ: Prentice-Hall, 1968.

Lee, Richard Borshay. *The !Kung San: Men, Women, and Work in a Foraging Society.* Cambridge: Cambridge University Press, 1979.

Lewis, David. *Convention: A Philosophical Study.* Cambridge, Mass.: Harvard University Press, 1969.

Lewis, Oscar. *Life in a Mexican Village: Tepoztlán Restudied.* Urbana, Ill.: University of Illinois Press, 1951.

Lienhardt, Godfrey. 'The situation of death: an aspect of Anuak philosophy', in M. Douglas, ed., *Witchcraft Accusations and Confessions.* London: Tavistock, 1970.

Loehr, William, and Sandler, Todd, eds. *Public Goods and Public Policy.* Beverly Hills: Sage, 1978.

Lovins, Amory. *Soft Energy Paths.* Harmondsworth: Penguin, 1977.

Lukes, Steven. *Power: A Radical View.* London: Macmillan, 1974.

Malinowski, Bronislaw. *Argonauts of the Western Pacific.* London: Routledge and Kegan Paul, 1922.

Crime and Custom in Savage Society. London: Routledge and Kegan Paul, 1926.

Marshall, Lorna. 'Sharing, talking, and giving: relief of social tensions among !Kung Bushmen', *Africa,* 31 (1961), 231–49.

Mauss, Marcel. *The Gift: Forms and Functions of Exchange in Archaic Societies.* London: Routledge and Kegan Paul, 1969.

Midgley, Mary. *Beast and Man.* London: Methuen, 1980.

Miller, David. *Social Justice.* Oxford: Clarendon Press, 1976.

Montagu, Ashley, ed. *Learning Non-Aggression.* New York: Oxford University Press, 1978.

Morgan, Lewis Henry. *Ancient Society.* Cambridge, Mass.: Harvard University Press, 1964.

Nadel, S. F. 'Social control and self-regulation', *Social Forces,* 3 (1953), 265–73.

Nagel, Thomas. 'Libertarianism without foundations', *Yale Law Journal*, 85 (1975), 136–49.

Nash, Manning. 'The social context of economic choice in a small society', *Man*, 61 (1961), 186–91.

Netting, Robert McC. 'Sacred power and centralization: aspects of political adaptation in Africa', in B. Spooner, ed., *Population Growth: Anthropological Implications*. Cambridge, Mass.: MIT Press, 1972.

Nordhoff, Charles. *The Communistic Societies of the United States*. New York: Schocken, 1965.

Nozick, Robert. 'Coercion', in S. Morgenbesser, P. Suppes and M. White, eds., *Philosophy, Science and Method: Essays in Honor of Ernest Nagel*. New York: St Martin's Press, 1969. Reprinted in P. Laslett, W. G. Runciman and Q. Skinner, eds., *Philosophy, Politics and Society*, Fourth Series. Oxford: Blackwell, 1972.

Anarchy, State and Utopia. Oxford: Blackwell, 1974.

Oliver, Douglas. *A Solomon Island Society*. Cambridge, Mass.: Harvard University Press, 1955.

Olson, Mancur. *The Logic of Collective Action*. Cambridge, Mass.: Harvard University Press, 1965.

O'Neill, Onora. 'Nozick's entitlements', *Inquiry*, 19 (1976), 468–81.

Oppenheim, Felix E. *Dimensions of Freedom*. New York: St Martin's Press, 1961.

Orlove, Benjamin. 'Inequality among peasants: the forms and uses of reciprocal exchange in Andean Peru', in R. Halperin and J. Dow, eds., *Peasant Livelihood: Studies in Economic Anthropology and Cultural Ecology*. New York: St Martin's Press, 1977.

Otterbein, K. F., and Otterbein, C. S. 'An eye for an eye, a tooth for a tooth: a cross-cultural study of feuding', *American Anthropologist*, 67 (1965), 1470–82.

Pateman, Carole. *Participation and Democratic Theory*. Cambridge: Cambridge University Press, 1970.

The Problem of Political Obligation: A Critical Analysis of Liberal Theory. London: Wiley, 1979.

Peters, R. S. 'Freedom and the development of the free man', in J. F. Doyle, ed., *Educational Judgements: Papers in the Philosophy of Education*. London: Routledge and Kegan Paul, 1973.

Polanyi, Karl; Arensberg, Conrad M.; and Pearson, Harry W., eds., *Trade and Market in the Early Empires*. Glencoe, Ill.: Free Press, 1957.

Popkin, Samuel L. *The Rational Peasant*. Berkeley: University of California Press, 1979.

Pospisil, Leopold. *Kapauku Papuans and their Law*. Yale University Publications in Anthropology no. 54. New Haven, Conn.: Yale University Press, 1958.

Radcliffe-Brown, A. R. *The Andaman Islanders*. Cambridge: Cambridge University Press, 1922.

Rapoport, Roy A. 'The sacred in human evolution', *Annual Review of Ecology and Systematics,* 2 (1971), 23–44.

Reay, Marie. *The Kuma: Freedom and Conformity in the New Guinea Highlands*. Melbourne: University Press, 1959.

Richards, Audrey. *Land, Labour and Diet in Northern Rhodesia*. 2nd edition. London: Oxford University Press, 1961.

Ritter, Archibald. *The Economic Development of Revolutionary Cuba*. New York: Praeger, 1974.

Rodgers, James D. 'Explaining income redistribution', in H. H. Hochman and G. E. Peterson, eds., *Redistribution Through Public Choice*. New York: Columbia University Press, 1974.

Rothbard, Murray. *For a New Liberty; the Libertarian Manifesto*. Revised edition. New York: Collier, 1978.

Ryan, Cheyney C. 'Yours, mine and ours: property rights and individual liberty', *Ethics,* 87 (1976–7), 126–41.

Sahlins, Marshall. 'The segmentary lineage: an organization of predatory expansion', *American Anthropologist,* 63 (1961), 332–45.

'Poor man, rich man, big-man, chief: political types in Melanesia and Polynesia', *Comparative Studies in Society and History,* 5 (1963), 285–303.

Stone Age Economics. London: Tavistock, 1974.

Schwartz, Richard D. 'Social control in two Israeli settlements', in D. Black and M. Mileski, eds., *The Social Organization of Law*. New York: Seminar Press, 1973.

Scott, James C. *The Moral Economy of the Peasant: Rebellion and Subsistence in Southeast Asia*. New Haven, Conn.: Yale University Press, 1976.

Service, Elman R. *Origins of the State and Civilization*. New York: Norton, 1975.

Shambaugh, Bertha M. *Amana That Was and Amana That Is*. Iowa City: State Historical Society of Iowa, 1932.

Shanin, Teodor. *The Awkward Class*. Oxford: Clarendon Press, 1972.

'The nature and logic of the peasant economy', Part I, *Journal of Peasant Studies,* 1 (1973), 63–80.

Skocpol, Theda. *States and Social Revolutions*. Cambridge: Cambridge University Press, 1979.

Smith, M. G. 'On segmentary lineage systems', *Journal of the Royal Anthropological Institute,* 86 (1956), 39–80.

Southall, Adrian. 'Stateless society', *International Encyclopedia of the Social Sciences* (1968), vol. 15, pp. 157–68.

Spencer, Robert F. *The North Alaskan Eskimo: A Study in Ecology and Society*. Smithsonian Institution Bureau of American Ethnology

Bulletin 171. Washington, DC: US Government Printing Office, 1959.

Spiro, Melford. *Kibbutz: Venture in Utopia*. New York: Schocken, 1963.

Stauder, Jack. 'Anarchy and ecology: political society among the Majangir', *Southwestern Journal of Anthropology*, 28 (1972), 153–68.

Steiner, Hillel. 'Individual liberty', *Proceedings of the Aristotelian Society*, NS, 75 (1974–5), 33–50.

Swanson, Guy E. *The Birth of the Gods*. Ann Arbor: Michigan University Press, 1960.

Taylor, Michael. *Anarchy and Cooperation*. London and New York: Wiley, 1976.

Thoden van Velzen, H. U. E., and Wetering, W. van. 'Residence, power groups and intra-societal aggression', *International Archives of Ethnography*, 49 (1960), 169–200.

Thurow, Lester C. 'The income distribution as a public good', *Quarterly Journal of Economics*, 85 (1971), 327–33.

Tilly, Charles. 'Reflections on the history of European state-making', in C. Tilly, ed., *The Formation of National States in Western Europe*. Princeton, NJ: Princeton University Press, 1975.

Turnbull, Colin. *The Forest People*. London: Jonathan Cape, 1961.

Turner, Victor W. *The Ritual Process*. Chicago: Aldine, 1969.

Tylor, Edward B. 'On a method of investigating the development of institutions: applied to laws of marriage and descent', *Journal of the Royal Anthropological Institute*, 18 (1888), 245–67.

Varian, Hal R. 'Equity, envy and efficiency', *Journal of Economic Theory*, 9 (1974), 63–91.

'Distributive justice, welfare economics and the theory of fairness', *Philosophy and Public Affairs*, 4 (1974–5), 223–47.

Waismann, F. *How I See Philosophy*. London: Macmillan, 1968.

Weber, Max. *Economy and Society*. Vol. 1, edited by G. Roth and C. Wittich. New York: Bedminster Press, 1968.

Webster, D. 'Warfare and the evolution of the state: a reconsideration', *American Antiquity*, 40 (1975), 464–70.

Weinstein, W. L. 'The concept of liberty in nineteenth century English political thought', *Political Studies*, 13 (1963), 145–62.

Whyte, Martin King. *Small Groups and Political Rituals in China*. Berkeley: University of California Press, 1974.

Williams, Aaron. *The Harmony Society at Economy, Pennsylvania*. Pittsburgh: W. S. Haven, 1866.

Wilson, Monica. *Good Company: A Study of Nyakyusa Age-Villages*. London: Oxford University Press, 1951.

Wolf, Eric R. 'Types of Latin American peasantry: a preliminary discussion', *American Anthropologist*, 57 (1955), 452–71.

'Closed corporate peasant communities in Mesoamerica and Central Java', *Southwestern Journal of Anthropology,* 13 (1957), 1–18.

Peasants. Englewood Cliffs, NJ: Prentice-Hall, 1966.

Young, Michael W. *Fighting With Food.* Cambridge: Cambridge University Press, 1971.

Young, T. Culyer, Jr. 'Population densities in early Mesopotamian urbanism', in P. J. Ucko, *et al.*, eds., *Man, Settlement and Urbanism.* London: Duckworth, 1972.

Zablocki, Benjamin. *The Joyful Community: An Account of the Bruderhof, a Communal Movement Now in its Third Generation.* Baltimore: Penguin, 1971.

Index